Your Invisible Toolbox

Your Invisible Toolbox

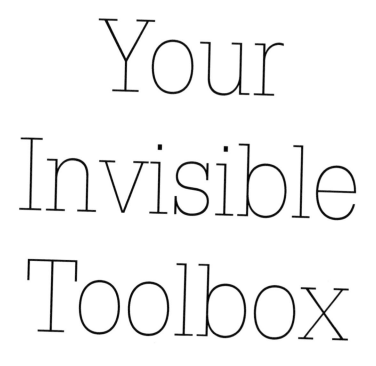

THE
TECHNOLOGICAL UPS AND
INTERPERSONAL DOWNS OF THE
MILLENNIAL GENERATION

bpc

Business Publications Corporation Inc.

Your Invisible Toolbox is published by Business Publications Corporation Inc., an Iowa corporation.

Copyright © 2017 by Rowena Crosbie and Deborah Rinner.

ISBN-13: 978-0-9986528-0-1
Library of Congress Control Number: 2017905883
Business Publications Corporation Inc., Des Moines, IA

bpc

Business Publications Corporation Inc.
The Depot at Fourth
100 4th Street
Des Moines, Iowa 50309
(515) 288-3336

For Ted and Charles

Your belief in the potential of people
and passion for developing future generations
has been an inspiration.

It's all possible. Your legacies live on.

About the Artist

Kevin Wilson was born in Winnipeg, Manitoba, in 1967 and is currently living in Edmonton, Alberta. He also happens to be the brother of Rowena Crosbie, one of the authors of Your Invisible Toolbox. It was during his high school years when Kevin discovered his talent to create. From there, he started teaching himself the techniques of airbrush painting. He honed his craft by starting on canvas, slowly graduating from there to motorcycles, helmets, vehicles and anything that could be painted.

In 2013, Kevin partnered with two local artists from Winnipeg and created The Creative Collective art group. For two years, they have executed art shows that showcase various independent local artists – including everything from tattoo artists to mixed media artists producing work out of their home. Kevin's work has been featured in art shows throughout Canada, including the 2015 Art Walk in Edmonton and the 2016 Lab Art Show and the Art World Expo, both in Vancouver. Additionally, Kevin has received various honors for his airbrush work on motorcycles.

Kevin's preferred medium has always been metal, anything from steel to aluminum. His newest pieces consist of a collaboration of shapes and colors and custom airbrushing. Kevin's work is freehand, original and always exploring new approaches. The piece that was created for the cover of this book is custom and of the same title, Your Invisible Toolbox. It is painted on a 4-foot by 4-foot sheet of aluminum that was cut specifically for this work. The two faces are also cut from metal and attached to the base, making the art piece three-dimensional. The toolbox that connects the two individuals is subtle, reflecting the nature of interpersonal tools that remain in the background in positive human interactions. The color and visual experience change in different lighting due to a grinding process that preceded the airbrush work and the use of candy urethane paint to capture the bright colors. The original artwork hangs in the Tero International headquarters in Des Moines, Iowa.

Contents

Foreword

Millennials, Generation Y, or Echo Boomers are some of the common names given to the American population born between the 1980s and early 2000s. Never a day goes by when the public does not read or hear about the work ethics, behavior, and attitudes of millennials that differ from the generations preceding them. Demographers state that this cohort is the largest population group ever to enter the labor force at one time in the history of this country. It is estimated that by the year 2020, there will be nearly 86 million millennials in the workplace—or 40 percent of the total working population.

Being the first generation to enter the workforce in the twenty-first century, millennials are the most popular subjects to observe and evaluate. Their lives are transformed by multiple factors, including social, economic, and technological, that were unknown and almost nonexistent in the lives of generation X and the baby boomers. Consequently, this impact has generated a paradigm shift in the values, attitudes, and social and interpersonal skills of millennials at work.

Some of the hallmark qualities that have been observed of millennials are technical adeptness, innovativeness, and entrepreneurial skills. They are known to be confident, self-assured, decisive, and extremely well informed. In a detailed and comprehensive article, *Time* magazine described millennials as those who "might be the new greatest generation."

According to the Pew Research Center, millennials should be recognized for being multitaskers, well informed, and civic-minded. However, the observations also indicate that millennials have been perceived as being self-obsessed, self-promotional through social media, and short on social skills: "They do not retain information; they spend most of their energy sharing short social messages, being entertained, and being distracted away from deep engagement with people and knowledge. They lack face-to-face social skills…"

The Pew Research Center study concluded that millennials benefit but also suffer due to their hyperconnected lives.

The twenty-first-century professional faces multiple challenges in the job market. High-tech proficiency and hard-core skills are necessary and valued, but professionals also need to be adept in soft skills. At work, we have to deal with people, and that necessitates the need to be proficient in interpersonal skills.

Tero International has been a leading interpersonal research, design and training firm for over two decades. This book provides a compilation of the knowledge and expertise gathered through experience, putting it into the hands of everyone, but particularly the millennials. This book poses the dilemmas, questions, and conflicts millennials face and provides the interpersonal tools necessary for them and all of us to succeed.

Coupled with the advantages millennials bring to the workplace, by enhancing their interpersonal communication skills through *Your Invisible Toolbox*, millennials may turn out to be, as *Time* magazine mentioned, the "new greatest generation."

Harwant Khush, Ph.D.

Preface

In a very real sense, Rowena Crosbie and Deborah Rinner are like sculptors of the Renaissance who are producing great works of art. However, their finished products are not static marble figures to be displayed in museums to impress visitors, but rather dynamic interactive millennial professionals trained to impact their clients and collaborators.

In their new volume, *Your Invisible Toolbox*, "Ro" and "Deb" have distilled twenty-five years of enormously successful professional training at Tero International, the "go-to" institute in Central Iowa for turning out polished performers, from Miss America contestants to entry-level agricultural extension specialists and future corporate boardroom occupants.

With one hundred compelling stories, each sharing an insight into more effective interpersonal interaction, *Your Invisible Toolbox* is based on the bottom-line proposition that 85 percent of career success depends on soft skills. Whether coaching on making eye contact, business etiquette, or effective public speaking, the authors provide two- or three-word bottom-line lessons and insights that are designed as takeaways to put the finishing touches on an entire generation of newly minted young professionals.

Each of the one hundred stories, from number 1, "It Was One of Those Days," to the concluding "Are You Who You Say You Are?", has such an engaging title that addressing the table of contents is akin to being offered a piece of candy from a box of spectacularly tempting chocolates: You don't know where to start, but you feel assured that whichever you pick, it will be delicious. And the one thing that is certain is that it will leave you wanting more. They are so irresistible, you can't ingest just one.

Indeed, the stories are so succinct and the bottom-line takeaway aphorisms so pithy that each could be printed on a card, somewhat like the classy notes left on your pillow at a boutique hotel. It could provide a one-a-day lesson with a two- or three-word bottom line that would only take five to ten minutes to ingest and be easy to remember and practice the following day but impart an invisible "tool" that will last a lifetime.

Given my thirty-two-year career at the US State Department, including an assignment at the National Security Council of the White House, I naturally gravitated to stories like number 31, "The White House Crashers," and number 52, "The Everyday Diplomat," in the section entitled "Tools for Working Globally." I came away wishing that *Your Invisible Toolbox* had been available at the Foreign Service Institute when I went through my own entry-level training for a diplomatic career.

Ambassador Kenneth M. Quinn (ret.)
President, World Food Prize Foundation

Acknowledgments

Special acknowledgment and thanks to the Tero International staff, trainers, consultants, and interns for their important roles in the research, development, customization, and delivery of Tero training programs, for their efforts in data collection, analysis, and interpretation, and for valuable contributions to the content in this book.

Sincere thanks also to the Tero clients who have placed their trust and confidence in the Tero Team to help them build the competitive advantage that comes from mastery of the interpersonal skills used in business.

We also thank the many individuals who generously gave of their time to review an early copy of the book and provide their impressions. Several of their comments have been included in this book.

Deep-felt appreciation to Ashley Holter and the team at Business Publications for their work in bringing this project to readers and special thanks to Renee Johnson who skillfully edited the book.

Finally, we are indebted to Kevin Wilson whose artistic talents created the inspiring image which graces the cover of this book. Kevin's artwork expertly captures the book's theme. The essential tools for improving communications and relationships are available to all if we just look hard enough to find them and work hard enough to master their use.

Introduction

Each of us has two sets of tools. The first toolbox is filled with the technical skills, equipment, and devices needed to help us carry out our activities. The second toolbox is invisible. It contains the tools that we use in human interactions.

How important are the tools in the invisible toolbox?

Microsoft has not yet invented the software that calms an irate customer, juggles multiple and conflicting priorities, and collaborates with team members to solve a complex problem—all on the same day. Apple has not yet designed the device that negotiates conflict with a colleague, demonstrates compassion to a loved one, extends kindness to a stranger, or mentors a protégé.

Those tasks are handled by people relying on the tools contained in their invisible toolboxes. When we use the tools effectively, relationships flourish, businesses grow, and personal happiness results. When we use the tools ineffectively, relationships are damaged, businesses suffer, and personal hardship results.

Highly developed interpersonal skills have never been more important. Relating well to others is increasingly a casualty of our high-tech world that brings us smaller and smaller devices and fewer and fewer opportunities to master the complex skills of human relations.

While the tools in the second toolbox are invisible, the effects are profound. According to Harvard University, Stanford Research Institute, and the Carnegie Foundation, technical skills account for 15 percent of the reason we get a job, keep a job, and advance in a job. The other 85 percent of our success comes from our use of the tools in our invisible toolbox.

Working across geographies and industries with groups and individuals for over two decades has afforded the authors of this book a unique opportunity. We have seen firsthand the interpersonal dilemmas, struggles, problems, and decisions facing business professionals. The tools in *Your Invisible Toolbox* were forged from what we have learned works, and they reflect what is necessary for everyone to have on hand in order to effectively relate, connect, understand, and lead.

The First One Hundred Days

The phrase "the first one hundred days" is widely acknowledged as a period of time in which someone new to a role strives to learn his or her responsibilities and form a unique approach to work. Whether a new CEO, a new hire, or someone accepting a new role, the first one hundred days is commonly known as the honeymoon period where judgments from others are often withheld to allow time for the individual to settle into his or her role.

It is in the spirit of the first one hundred days that we've written this book. Although useful to every generation in the workplace, it is designed with the millennial business professional in mind. Although the invisible tools are useful for anyone, the millennial generation has unprecedented challenges when it comes to the need for these tools.

The ability of millennials to positively affect business and relationships in ways no other generation has before them is evident. The rapid pace of change and technological advances minimizing human connection place them at risk. To leverage technology and change to yield its greatest potential for the future, millennials must utilize a full toolbox of interpersonal effectiveness tools.

Millennials may not be given a formal hundred-day grace period to develop the interpersonal capacity necessary for their advancing roles and increased responsibilities.

This book provides millennials, and all of us, an extended honeymoon period in which to develop interpersonal effectiveness. Divided into five parts, it encompasses one hundred chapters, each providing a critical interpersonal tool for success in the workplace.

When used well, the effects of using these tools are anything but invisible.

Part I

TOOLS FOR INTERACTING WITH OTHERS

An interest in mastering the skills and tools of human relations in business is nothing new. What is new is how complex the environment is for businesses today. In a high-tech interconnected world, the challenge is greater and the stage is bigger. In the past, communication was largely one-way and change occurred at a manageable pace. Technology changed all that.

Business is changing, and traditional education has not prepared professionals for this new reality. The skills that led to success in the past are being challenged and replaced with new models of interacting. The business people who will succeed in this new economy are those who master a new set of skills for interacting effectively with others.

In this part of the book, we examine the tools for interacting effectively with others.

I've learned that you shouldn't go through life with a catcher's mitt on both hands; you need to be able to throw something back.
MAYA ANGELOU

1

IT WAS ONE OF THOSE DAYS

A Pew Research Center study reported that 59 percent of millennials described their own generation as self-absorbed. Forty-three percent said they were greedy. Many don't like being identified as millennials, and 60 percent don't consider themselves to be a part of the millennial generation.

"He said, 'Just do it for somebody else.' That's when it dawned on me that it was one of those pay-it-forward scenarios and that it would mean a lot to him if I accepted."

It was one of those days. It was November 10, 2015. Jamie-Lynne Knighten had just returned from a visit with family in her native Ontario, Canada. Now she, her husband, and young children were back in their new San Diego, California, home, and she was picking up groceries at a supermarket.

She had taken her youngest child with her to the store. The five-month-old was being fussy. The shopping excursion took an hour and a half. When Jamie reached the checkout, she realized she had forgotten her debit card at home.

The grocery total was more than $200. She remembered she had her Canadian credit card with her. Jamie gave the cash she had on hand to the cashier and swiped her Canadian credit card. Declined. She swiped it again. Declined. She surmised that they had put an anti-fraud lock on the card because of her travels, and she called the credit card company to have it lifted. Her phone died. A line was forming behind her at the checkout. She was trying to hold it together.

It was one of those days.

"Take us back to the day in the grocery store. How did you come to meet?" was the question posed to Jamie-Lynne Knighten by CBC Radio

As It Happens host Carol Off. Jamie recalled that she was about to ask the cashier if they could hold her purchases so she could return home to fetch her debit card when a stranger's voice said, "May I?"

"May you what?" she replied.

"May I take care of your groceries?"

She protested with her thanks. After all, it was a large purchase, and this was a stranger.

The stranger replied, "I would like to. Do me one thing. Just do it for somebody else." Jamie realized he was serious and that this was a pay-it-forward gesture. She accepted.

As they left the store, she introduced herself and learned the young man who had performed this random act of kindness was named Matthew. She shared with Matthew that her family had just moved to the area and that she was feeling a little overwhelmed. She inquired where he worked, and he responded, "LA Fitness." Jamie promised herself that she would follow up with Matthew in the days ahead to thank him more formally.

It would be another week before she learned that Matthew's last name was Jackson. That he was twenty-eight years old. That he died in a car accident on November 11, 2015.

Jamie had called the local gym about a week after the encounter and spoke with Matthew's manager in hopes of reaching him and reconnecting. It was through tears that his manager told her about the tragedy.

When Jamie called her husband to tell him the sad news, it hit him hard. The stereotypical US Marine, who doesn't get upset about too many things, was shaken by the news. It was a cold reminder of how fragile life is.

Jamie came to know about Matthew and his character from his boss, who had worked with him for four years. She told Jamie, "That's who he was. Always doing for other people. Never asking for anything in return." Through his coworkers, Jamie was able to connect with Matthew's mother and spent two hours discovering more about who Matthew Jackson was.

"She told me he was a big sweetheart who was always doing things for other people. One thing she's really proud of is that he's a bear hugger. In every photo you see of him with somebody, he doesn't just have one arm around them. He's giving them a huge bear hug. And that's what it felt like when he paid for my groceries and took care of me."

Jamie created a Facebook page called *Matthew's Legacy*, asking people to do something extraordinary for a stranger to honor Matthew and help restore faith in humanity. The response has been worldwide, and the stories are heartwarming. Jamie says she wants her children "to recognize that they can actively participate in making a positive change in the world like he did." She goes on to say, "It doesn't have to be monetary. It doesn't have to be huge and grandiose. Create a lifestyle of kindness. Help people in small ways or big ways. Whatever you can do. Every little bit helps."

YOUR INVISIBLE TOOLBOX

Matthew's legacy endures, and Jamie is paying it forward. This is a powerful lesson for you to contemplate as it challenges the labels often ascribed to millennials of self-absorbed and greedy. This is one excellent example of the interest millennials claim they have for their fellow humans being translated into action. When have you missed the opportunity to perform a random act of kindness?

Surprise someone with kindness

2

THE HOPEFUL GENERATION

In 2014 the deficit in civility perceived by the generations looked like this:

- Millennials (93 percent)
- Gen Xers (92 percent)
- Boomers (94 percent)
- Silent Generation (97 percent)

Almost one in four millennials (23 percent) believed civility would improve in the next few years. Has it? Is the hope of this generation founded in experience?

Millennials, the largest cohort generation in the workforce, value civility. Why is that view and outlook so important?

It's not difficult to appreciate the benefit of taking the time to intentionally show gratitude to people in our family and social circles. We readily engage in reciprocity, giving thanks and acknowledgment to effectively support and maintain the people and personal relationships we hold most important to us.

What about in the workplace? Where business is the bottom line, do we need to take the time to intentionally thank the coworkers we interact with? Does gratitude create a workplace benefit? If it does, how do we make sure we're taking the opportunities to demonstrate it enough and appropriately?

Dr. P. M. Forni of Johns Hopkins University has alluded that showing thanks in the workplace is not only important, it is imperative to the health of an organization. Dr. Forni is head of the Johns Hopkins Civility Initiative and has conducted numerous studies to assess the effect of civility in the workplace. Not only have the findings concluded that treating coworkers politely lowers stress (which can activate positive rather than negative effects in the nervous and immune systems), but civility also positively influences tenure, absenteeism, and workplace morale.

Unfortunately, while civility is often valued in organizational missions, it isn't always evident in day-to-day interactions. A solution to demonstrating civility in the workplace can be as simple as remembering to intentionally acknowledge others and give written thanks.

Psychologist and philosopher William James said the "deepest principle in human nature is the craving to be appreciated." It may be challenging to remain aware of the many tasks and responsibilities we engage in during the workday. It's easy to remember the activities that coworkers intentionally thank us for. Receiving acknowledgment and thanks influences not only our sense of contribution to our organization but fuels our desire to further contribute.

Although our responsibilities in our job may solely be our own, on any given day there are numerous "behind the scenes" people who make what we do possible. This list can begin with the person who cleaned the workroom sink or makes the coffee all the way to the CEO who is ever pitching and visioning so we maintain our livelihood. If we really stopped to count the number of people who positively affect what we can accomplish in a single day, we would likely be surprised at how many there are—and how rarely we intentionally show appreciation.

The metaphoric words of author Peggy Tabor Millin describe the benefit and results of being intentional with our thanks.

"I was on a train on a rainy day. The train was slowing down to pull into a station. For some reason, I became intent on watching the raindrops on the window. Two separate drops, pushed by the wind, merged into one for a moment and divided again—each carrying a part of the other. Simply by that momentary touching, neither was what it had been before. And as each went on to touch other raindrops, it shared not only itself, but what it had gleaned from the other. I realized that we never touch people so lightly that we do not leave a trace. We need to become conscious of what we unintentionally share, so we learn to share with intention."

YOUR INVISIBLE TOOLBOX

Civility involves thinking of others as much as ourselves. Is there a person you are thinking of right now whom you appreciate? Maybe the person assists your efforts in the workplace or influences who you are becoming as a professional? If so, take a minute to write a brief personal note to this person, intentionally telling him or her the things he or she does that matter to you.

Write a personal note

3

I KNOW EXACTLY WHAT HAPPENED

Most millennials share stories, images, and facts about their lives on social media. The movement started with Facebook and has evolved as platforms like YouTube, Instagram, and Snapchat arrived on the scene. We are all part of a movement where everything we think, say, and do can be tweeted, posted, and blogged for public consumption. When does sharing become over-sharing? Is there a line?

Be careful with your words; once they are said,
they can be only forgiven, not forgotten.
UNKNOWN

It is said that customers measure a company not by how they are treated when things go smoothly but by how they are treated when problems with its product or service arise. It is in these moments that customers decide who they will flatter with their future business.

The scene is familiar. A group of passengers is milling around the airport boarding gate awaiting word on the status of their delayed flight. Boarding can't commence because the copilot has not arrived.

Federal Aviation Authority guidelines prohibit a pilot from flying alone. Calls have been made to the copilot's home, but he can't be located.

Everyone waits.

Apparently the copilot called in three days earlier to book the day off. Someone failed to replace him on the schedule. The flight is due to leave Los Angeles on New Year's Day. Some of the travelers surmise the copilot is at the Rose Bowl.

Three hours later, when the passengers finally board their flight, crew members are asked, "What happened?"

Following are their responses. Imagine you are a senior leader in this organization. Two of your company's values are honesty and good customer service. How does the customer experience measure up?

1. "A new crew had to be called in. We're doing the best we can."
2. "We had to take a thirty-five percent pay cut, and everybody is calling in sick in protest. I was called in to replace them. I've worked every holiday this year."
3. "On behalf of all of us at the airline, I apologize for this unbelievable situation. We know this is an inconvenience for you. I've worked for this airline for twenty-four years and have never seen a scheduling oversight like this. We are embarrassed and appreciate your patience. We will get you to your destination as soon as possible."

All three responses pass the honesty test. However, handling customer communications during a difficult time requires more than just an honest answer. It also requires:

- Discretion. While you must be 100 percent truthful (customers do not tolerate dishonesty), you do not have to be 100 percent open. Your principal tactical challenge is to determine how open you should be. The reputation of the organization is entrusted to the individuals who communicate with customers.

- Expressing compassion. While challenging, it is important to address the issue from the viewpoint of the customer, not your company or yourself. That is the viewpoint they will be listening from.

Three honest answers. The differences relate to discretion and compassion. Response (1) was impersonal and defensive. Response (2) revealed troubling morale issues. Only (3) began to address the issue from the customer's viewpoint.

YOUR INVISIBLE TOOLBOX

Customer service is high on the list of key differentiators and competitive advantage for organizations, including this airline. This uncommon skill is too often left to chance. The good news is that the skills of good customer communication are learned. Always consider the audience, use discretion, and express compassion when communicating, especially when the news is bad.

Be discreet and compassionate

THE BIG ASK

October 4, 2014 turned out to be an interesting day for Satya Nadella, CEO of Microsoft. When presenting at a computing conference attended by 7,500 female engineers, he was asked to give advice to women who are afraid to ask for a raise. He suggested they work hard and trust karma.

As you can imagine, this advice, in an age of documented social, economic, political, and cultural issues affecting how women are perceived and misperceived in the workplace, didn't go over too well.

Most of us would agree that cause can influence effect (karma), yet given the business landscape women travail, peppered as it is with gender-ridden landmines, just trying hard and waiting for someone to notice is not enough.

Unfortunately, just asking isn't enough either.

In a perfect world, productive work by males and females would be equally noticed and rewarded. In a perfect world, women and men would feel correspondingly comfortable and competent asking for a raise or promotion if there is due contribution meriting one.

The question asked of Nadella, as well as the answer reveal what we already know. It is not yet a perfect world in the workplace for women… or men, for that matter.

We need to stop buying into the myth about gender equality.
It isn't a reality yet. Today, women make up half of the US workforce,
but the average working woman earns only 77 percent of what the average
working man makes. But unless women and men both say
this is unacceptable, things will not change.
BEYONCÉ

Nadella apologized a few days later, stating he realized his answer didn't include the information that he supports programs to close the pay gap between men and women. He made it clear he should have said that when women think they deserve a raise they should just ask for one. In the aftermath of his initial remarks, he became conscious of the fact that karma may be skewed due to gender. But did he realize the advice to "just ask" might be skewed as well?

It is commonly cited that:
- Women don't ask.
- Women should ask.
- Women have to be careful how to ask.
- A woman's risk in asking might be greater than the benefit— if the ask doesn't go well.

Obviously the issue is complicated for everyone involved, women and men.

It's indisputable that there's a real pay gap.
People can argue about how big, but that's almost beside the point.
The point is that every woman, every girl, deserves to
get paid what they're worth.
SHERYL SANDBERG

The gender disparity in comfort and response with regard to asking for a raise is evident. But even if it wasn't there, do both men and women communicate interests in a way that influences thought, creates buy in, and reflects value to the other party involved?

Too often when trying to influence a decision during communication we focus on short-term tangible results. An immediate pay increase is a short-term tangible. We set that request on the table, and whomever we are asking responds in kind. Your short-term tangible may be the raise. Your employer's short-term tangible interest may be profit margin for this quarter.

Battling around in the short-term tangible realm creates opposition quicker than buy in.

In the world of interests, there are more than short-term tangibles (things that can be measured). With respect to a raise, you are asking for the raise not just for the short-term tangible money, but also for the intangible feelings and attitudes that are important to you, such as recognition of your work. In the long term, the tangible raise is an indicator of a healthy career or a path toward managing. In the long-term intangible, the interest could mean security or reputation as a leader.

There are four types of interests, short-term, long-term, tangible, and intangible. To be successful influencing a decision, and to make points that signal common gain, it is crucial while asking not to stay in the short-term tangible box of dollars and cents. You need to communicate what your request means in terms of recognition, career goals, and aspirations. These are the intangible and long-term considerations that benefit everyone.

YOUR INVISIBLE TOOLBOX

Linking intangibles and long-term interests to how the company can gain, as well as documenting contributions that illustrate evidence of these intents, is a much more influential way to handle the "big ask."

Address intangibles and the long term

5

A NEW WORLD OF CITIZEN JOURNALISM

"Don't tell anyone I told you..." We all say things when we don't think someone else is listening. How many of us have said something in the privacy of our homes or behind closed doors that we would be mortified if someone in an external audience heard it?

Members of the millennial generation are beginning and advancing their careers during the rise of a new trend in journalism. It's called citizen journalism. Citizen journalism is the ability for the ordinary person to report information (or misinformation) to a wide audience in real time thanks to the availability and affordability of technology.

People are being tethered 24/7 to increasingly smaller technological devices with increasingly more powerful computing capabilities. The Internet, its blogs, search engines, and social media communities have put the power of information in the hands of consumers. Billions of devices around the world allow for message sharing and spin at a pace never imagined.

Many are finding out the hard way that communications that may have been appropriate behind closed doors are not appropriate on the global stage. Like it or not, it appears this is the new normal, and it is here to stay.

With technology and social media and citizen journalism,
every rock that used to go unturned is now being flipped, lit, and put on TV.
LZ GRANDERSON

It was reported that more than $2 billion was spent on the 2012 US presidential race. This is a sum exponentially greater than in any previous presidential campaign in history. Did the money make the difference?

"There are 47 percent of the people who will vote for the president no matter what. All right, there are 47 percent who are with him, who are dependent upon government, who believe that they are victims, who believe the government has a responsibility to care for them, who believe that they are entitled to health care, to food, to housing, to you-name-it—that that's an entitlement. And the government should give it to them. And they will vote for this president no matter what.... These are people who pay no income tax. My job is not to worry about those people. I'll never convince them they should take personal responsibility and care for their lives."

These words, uttered by presidential candidate Mitt Romney at a private fund-raiser, were caught on videotape and later obtained by the liberal magazine *Mother Jones*. It was this one internal message leaked out to an external audience that may go down in history as the single factor that swayed the election and cost Governor Romney the opportunity to serve as president.

Iowa Rep. Bruce Braley, a Democrat running for the US Senate seat vacated by retiring Iowa Democratic Senator Tom Harkin, speaking to a group of lawyers at a fund-raising event in Texas, was caught on videotape disparaging Iowa Senator Chuck Grassley as "a farmer from Iowa who never went to law school."

A later apology and Braley's insistence that he was the better candidate for Iowa farmers was not enough to unravel the damage to his campaign. He was defeated by his opponent, now US Senator Joni Ernst.

This is the world millennials came of age in. Wayback Machine, the website that contains an impressive historical record of virtually everything that has ever been on the Internet, makes it extraordinarily difficult to ever hide.

YOUR INVISIBLE TOOLBOX

Not only are communications almost always at risk of becoming public, permanent records mean that communications can come back and haunt professionals years or decades after the offending behavior. Even statements made on websites have an afterlife.

Consider the consequences

6

WHAT ARE WE OVERLOOKING?

Millennials have a deep interest in not only knowing what they're expected to do but also why it matters. This is a different perspective from previous generations of workers who commonly carried out the work they were instructed to do without a lot of questions.

What's driving this change?

- One explanation may be the measuring stick millennials use to measure productivity. Rather than considering the hours worked in a day as a measure of success, they look to the results of what they've actually done.
- Millennials, it seems, feel compelled to know that what they're doing has value, even in little things.

At the heart of both of these trends is the imperative for feedback. It is a myth that millennials only want positive feedback. While all of us like to hear nice things about ourselves, millennials also crave regular feedback that includes constructive critique.

Millennials are used to feedback. They not only received it from parents who provided frequent praise and encouragement to bolster self-esteem, they're accustomed to instant feedback from the video games they play, the text messages they send, and the computers they've grown up with. It's how they know they're doing well or how they find out if they need to shift their behaviors or approach.

We all need people who will give us feedback. That's how we improve.
BILL GATES

Receiving feedback is an art that few are highly skilled in. However, there's one tool in your invisible toolbox that's valuable in mastering this skill: the art of asking open-ended questions.

Asking open-ended questions allows others to provide you with information beyond the usual conversation starters. They can be used effectively when receiving feedback to learn more about underlying interests, areas of concern, and successes. Open-ended questions are the secret weapons of investigative reporters and begin most commonly with the words Who? What? Where? When? How? Why?

What if you don't agree with the feedback you receive? Can you challenge it? Should you challenge it?

Test questions are probing questions designed to test ideas or challenge assumptions. They are especially useful when you disagree with a point but don't want to disagree directly. They are an excellent tool in your invisible toolbox for handling tension effectively.

If your leader is pushing for something that you know won't address a key interest he or she raised earlier, instead of telling him or her that something's been forgotten, you can try a test question such as:

- What about our interest in...?
- How does that affect our goals around...?
- What are we overlooking?

Similarly, if a problem has occurred due to an error unrelated to you, instead of pointing it out and getting defensive, you can ask test questions or make open-ended statements to see if deeper analysis of the situation will reveal the underlying issue.

- Walk me through the situation from the beginning.
- When did we become aware of the issue?
- What happened next?

YOUR INVISIBLE TOOLBOX

Most of us engage in several rounds of point/counterpoint when challenging feedback we've received. Instead of trying to rush to your point and risk having the other person become defensive, you can use open-ended questions, test questions, or open-ended statements to understand the feedback and prevent the point/counterpoint discussion that may be unproductive and lead to tension.

Ask test questions

7

MAY I MAKE A SUGGESTION?

Millennials question their leaders and offer ideas and opinions at higher rates than seen previously in the workplace. It is not out of disrespect that they do this. They have a sincere interest in learning more and contributing to the organization. Since the leaders they're questioning are often members of earlier generations, the active sharing of ideas by millennials can be perceived as offensive. In fairness, remember that many of these leaders were raised in the "children should be seen and not heard" generation. Their negative reaction to unsolicited ideas, opinions, and feedback is understandable. What's a millennial to do?

While much of the blame may rest on leaders who seem closed to new and different ideas, you can improve the chances of getting your voice heard by how you introduce and present your ideas.

Permission-seeking questions deliver many benefits. They are deceptively simple and yet produce game-changing results when used effectively.

A permission-seeking question is designed to clear the way for a new train of thought by getting an affirmative response first.

The art and science of asking questions is the source of all knowledge.
THOMAS BERGER

Anyone who has difficulty having his or her voice heard loves the permission-seeking question. Rather than trying to talk over people or waiting for a lull in the conversation to interject a point, you can ask a brief closed-ended permission-seeking question. This allows you to change the subject, introduce a new topic, or make a point of your own. Examples include:

- May I share an idea?
- May I make a suggestion?

- Can I toss out an option that may work?
- May I share some information about…?
- Can I share a thought?

They can also be used to support another person while allowing you to emphasize a point that's been made. For example:

- Can I tell you why I like your idea?
- May I build on something you just said?
- Can I point out an area of shared interest?

It is important to use permission-seeking questions positively. When used to disagree with someone, the approach will mostly backfire. "Can I tell you what's wrong with your idea?" or "May I tell you why that won't work?" are examples of permission-seeking questions used poorly.

YOUR INVISIBLE TOOLBOX

The permission-seeking question will stop and redirect the conversation more effectively than any statement you have been trying to interject into the dialogue. When the attention has shifted to you, make your point.

Seek permission

8

INSTEAD OF MAKING YOUR CASE

The chances are excellent that you consider learning and growth opportunities to be as important a part of your compensation package as health insurance, flexible time, paid time off, and your 401K. If you're like many millennials, you may have even accepted a position that paid a little less than another one because it offered the opportunity for professional development and personal growth.

It's a rare organization that doesn't talk about the importance of people and helping them grow. Many of these same organizations fail to champion training opportunities for their employees. While frustrating for employees, the misalignment between words and deeds is understandable.

There is a significant cost to professional development. While it does beat the cost of losing employees and having to replace them, that fact often escapes leaders who are focused on short-term goals and lean budgets.

The Association for Talent Development reports that companies in the United States invest on average 4 percent of their payroll in training and development. That translates to an average direct spend of $2,000 per year for an employee earning $50,000 in annual salary. In terms of time, forty hours are the recommended number of training hours per year (2 percent of a full-time employee's year). If the individual is new to the role or if the job requirements have changed, a considerably greater investment in time and dollars may be required.

If your employer isn't making an investment in your career development and if you feel like most millennials that your college education didn't completely prepare you for the work world, you'll need the skills to facilitate a productive conversation. How can you persuade your leader that an investment in your development will be good for the company? This can be an especially difficult challenge if your leader has embraced the stereotype that millennials job hop and won't be around for the long run.

Your primary challenge is to guide their thinking. The skill of guiding thinking effectively has far more applications than the one described here. This is a tool in the invisible toolbox you're wise to keep handy every day.

We are always more convinced by our own observations than we are by statements made by others. This is also true of leaders. If you can get someone thinking more broadly about a subject, benefits may come up that you hadn't even considered.

How do you get leaders to begin thinking about the consequences of not investing in development? How do you get them thinking about the benefits of helping employees develop their skills and knowledge? Open-ended questions or statements can be used to direct thinking.

Judge a man by his questions rather than by his answers.
VOLTAIRE

Let's look at a few examples:

Instead of making a case and telling a leader that an investment in professional development will benefit the company in the long term, you can open the conversation with a question like one of the following:

- What benefits would the company see if employees were fully skilled in all aspects of jobs and didn't have to spend valuable time learning through trial and error on the job?
- What would it mean to the business if we didn't have to waste time and energy dealing with personality issues and conflicts?
- How do mistakes affect our reputation in the marketplace?
- What does it cost the business when employees delay taking action because they lack confidence in their skills and abilities?
- What would a fully skilled workforce mean to the business?

YOUR INVISIBLE TOOLBOX

Instead of arguing your case or making your point and hoping your leaders see the wisdom of it, you can help them arrive at a conclusion of their own by asking good questions. Use open-ended questions and statements to guide thinking when you're trying to persuade someone to think differently about a topic.

Guide thinking

9

WHAT IS YOUR EDGE?

Successful individuals are often referred to as having an "edge." Yet what does it really mean?

Authors Alan Lewis and Dan McKone in their book *Edge Strategy: A New Mindset for Profitable Growth* discuss 1930s ecologists' discovery of what they called the "edge" effect. The ecologists found quail, grouse, and game birds were more prevalent in areas of transition from one agricultural landscape to another than in single habitats.

Why?

These environments clearly contained more vegetation and greater diversity, which led to greater survival and abundance of species. The idea was furthered in the 1950s, and edge environments were labeled ecotones, defined as the space between two or more diverse communities. The sweet spot between one landscape and another, rich with what each has to offer, a combination of the best of two worlds.

So what do ecotones or edge effects have to do with you and your ability to achieve mutually beneficial outcomes?

When solving a problem or making a decision, people usually focus too much on themselves and their interests alone. Their interests become their positions. Two positions create opposition.

By taking a cue from science, you'll see that the sweet spot of success is the place between one landscape and another. In science it's called an ecotone. In interpersonal situations, where you're trying to solve a problem or make a decision, it's called common ground.

Collaboration is when magic is made with more than one person.
It's when more than one person finds common ground on the same page.
MICHAEL URIE

To find your edge, you need to put your position aside for a moment and identify why it's important to you. Then put on the other hat. What's the position of the other party? You may not know exactly, but you can speculate. Why might they want what they want? Once you've identified their probable interests, you'll most likely discover common ground.

Your edge opportunity is the shared spot, or common ground, between you and the other party. When you can start a discussion with what you share, it begins productively and collaboratively. This way you're working toward a solution in a manner that promotes shared value.

No man is an island. We all have edge opportunities when we are working together to find common ground. We can develop an edge mindset. Like estuary waters that combine the beauties of salt with fresh, our edge opportunities of common ground are rich. What they contain and represent to us make for far more desirable waters in which to succeed.

YOUR INVISIBLE TOOLBOX

Common ground is the interests you share with another party. You may have differing positions. If you can identify the whys of what each party wants, you'll most likely find common ground.

Find common ground

10

A HIGHER LEVEL

It has been estimated that millennials listen to 75 percent more music on a daily basis than baby boomers, who proudly boast the importance of the music their generation created.

Listening is important to everyone, yet it's something we all take for granted. Have you ever thought about what constitutes effective listening? How good are your listening skills? Who are the people you consider to be excellent listeners in your life? How many are on the list?

Most people cannot name more than two or three people they consider to be great listeners. Those they can name they hold in high esteem.

Sometimes we are great listeners. Sometimes (if we are honest with ourselves), we find that we've tuned in and out of a conversation and just hope we've retained enough to fake it when the other party stops talking and looks at us with that expectant look that says, "So what do you think?"

The most important thing in communication is hearing what isn't said.
PETER F. DRUCKER

As we grow, we are often given conflicting messages about how to listen effectively. Although most parents want their children to become effective listeners, few of them were ever taught how to listen themselves and are therefore unsure of how to teach their children. As a result, they tend to repeat the patterns passed down to them by their parents.

Even people who are skilled in listening are typically listening to respond (what am I going to say next?) rather than listening to understand. Listening to understand is a higher level of listening.

Listening effectively is a key to building strong relationships. We all intend to listen well. Why don't most of us listen more effectively?

YOUR INVISIBLE TOOLBOX

Listening is widely misunderstood. People assume that because they can hear they can listen well, or that listening is a passive activity. In reality, listening is an active sport.

Listen to understand

11

SAY IT AGAIN, SAM

Studies show millennials would rather text than have to listen to a recorded voice mail message. They would rather e-mail than meet face-to-face if possible. And their brains are developing differently than previous generations due to technology use.

Kirk Erickson of the Brain Aging & Cognition Health Lab at the University of Pittsburgh, says, "Excessive tech usage, according to leading scientific publications, atrophies the frontal lobe, breaking down ties between different parts of the brain. Too much technology use also shrinks the outermost part of the brain, making it more difficult to process information. This can affect the way people interact. You might see changes in your ability to regulate emotions, your ability to remember certain events, your ability to pay attention to different things." Erickson went on to say, "These things all together will certainly affect how you communicate with people."

Paying attention, regulating emotions, and remembering are all important to communication. But too often communication is viewed as what we say and what we hear. Yet true communicating is an exchange that relies on a process to create a synergy between two people, which creates something far more significant than the message itself.

Synergy happens when the response you receive from someone validates what you've said. It's not about agreement or someone's take on what you said. It's a response that indicates that you and your words are important. It's achieved through the process of paraphrasing and checking in.

Many a man would rather you heard his story than granted his request.
PHILLIP STANHOPE

In conversation, the process of paraphrasing encourages you to repeat what was said, ideally by using the same words or as close to the original message as possible. It is simply saying again what was just said.

Why should you do this? To message to the person you're communicating with that both what was said and he or she is important to you. You can check in by saying "Is that what you meant?" And then carry the conversation forward.

Oprah Winfrey, one of the great interviewers of our time, uses paraphrasing beautifully. This pattern and the result can be heard by listening to her interviews. After asking a question, she listens to the response. When the response is finished, there is a pause, and then in her deeply eloquent voice she simply repeats what was said. It's not hard to imagine how one might feel when after disclosing some personal fact or information, the first response is what was just said. Paraphrasing dignifies, elevates, and validates the point and the person.

YOUR INVISIBLE TOOLBOX

Paraphrasing can be used whenever you're listening. Instead of thinking about what you're going to say next, concentrate on the message being communicated. This allows you to then say it again and ask if you got the message right before carrying the conversation forward.

Paraphrase and check in

—————————— 12 ——————————

WHETHER YOU LIKE IT OR NOT

Millennials have been reported as wanting more praise than other generations and often shut down when criticized verbally. Parents and teachers of the past were more punishment focused, so criticism is familiar to boomers. As a millennial, you've received positive feedback your whole life. Why wouldn't you shut down when critiqued?

Criticism, like rain, should be gentle enough to nourish a man's growth without destroying his roots.
FRANK A. CLARK

Verbal criticism is a fact of daily life. Hardly a day goes by when we do not hear cynical remarks, sarcastic comments, or just plain negative feedback about our actions and behavior from colleagues, managers, or family members. If communicated properly and in a positive tone, criticism can definitely have a positive impact on the behavior and performance of its receiver.

However, it can also have a devastating impact if delivered with negative connotation that gives the impression of undermining the self-worth, dignity, and self-esteem of its recipients. Insulting, offensive, and disparaging remarks should be stated properly, without destroying the relationship between the criticizer and the receiver.

Dr. Mark Gorkin, known as the "Stress Doctor," isolated three facets that make a work environment dysfunctional. They all implicate criticism.

• The first is a destructive communication style. Any style that communicates aggressiveness is condescending.

• Second is communication that sets up superior/subordinate camps. Remarks like "You don't get paid to think" illustrate a criticism that defines status along with being critical.

· Third is any communication that is defensive in attitude. It may be dismissive in tone or convey little interest in the issue or person at hand.

The question is how to escape the vicious cycle of criticism and at the same time not be defensive in return. The most popular and contemporary technique to handle criticism is to be nondefensive. The basic tenets of this approach are to understand the issue, find some truth in what the criticizer has to say, work out a plan, and come to an agreement.

The Influence classes at Tero International teach a skill that is most difficult to employ: how to be an active listener. Active listening works in all situations and is especially useful when needing to respond to verbal criticism without resorting to being defensive.

Active listening requires you to seek to receive the message. It requires you to acknowledge the importance of the issue. That doesn't mean saying "I'm sorry" or "I understand." Neither of those responses is authentic and may indicate you agree or understand something that you don't.

If the criticizer is angry that you arrived late, you might say, "Being on time is important to both of us." By stating this, you acknowledge the issue is important. Instead of defending yourself with an explanation for your tardiness, you can ask open-ended questions to get more context on what the criticizer means as well as get him or her to think about how you're viewing the situation.

Instead of operating in denial and brushing off the criticism by saying "sticks and stones may break my bones but words will never hurt me," the best approach is one that allows you to sit down and talk… whether you like it or not.

YOUR INVISIBLE TOOLBOX

Criticism is always going to be a pervasive reality in your working life. You can learn how to deal with hostile and confrontational situations if you have the proper knowledge and techniques. The nondefensive approach that includes active listening and asking questions is one of the best methods to deal with a confrontational situation.

Listen actively

13

I DON'T UNDERSTAND WHAT YOU'RE SAYING

TBH, it is offensive to me. JK. I can't even.

If you're able to understand the previous line, you're probably a millennial. You know that TBH means "to be honest," JK means "just kidding," and I can't even means the speaker is losing patience, is annoyed about something, or is at a loss for words.

The generations that preceded millennials were cautioned to guard against communicating with acronyms and industry-specific terminology unless the terms were defined or explained. Technical experts frequently got the heat for speaking in this coded language. Although often guilty as charged, they were not the only offenders, and business professionals across all disciplines were coached to carefully consider the jargon they used when communicating.

> *Management is proving beyond a shadow of a doubt they don't*
> *have enough to do. So they've invented a new acronym.*
> CONNIE WILLIS

An entirely new way of communicating came with the digital age and the advent of texting. Beyond the offensive acronyms of the past, today's communication is even more heavily encoded with a mix of shorthand, abbreviations, conjoined words, and invented phrases.

If you've ever traveled to a country where the language is foreign to you, you know firsthand how tough it is to understand even the most basic things. It's also frustrating.

YOUR INVISIBLE TOOLBOX

Remember that the internal language of texting may be familiar to members of a single generation. For other business professionals, it's a foreign language and creates unnecessary barriers to communication.

Watch your language

14

WHAT'S IN A NAME?

Are you good at remembering names? Did you say "no" when you read that question?

Most of us feel we are not good at remembering names. In fact, we convince ourselves we aren't. We say things to ourselves like "I'm just not good at names" or "I cannot remember names." Telling ourselves we're not good at it reinforces the belief, and thus we don't even try.

Does it really matter?

Consider this true story.

A woman was invited to meet a first lady of the United States at an event with about forty other people. She was introduced to the first lady and made just a bit of small talk before the first lady went up on the stage to give her speech.

Eight years later, the same first lady (now a former first lady) was scheduled for another event. The woman who had been introduced to her was invited to the gathering, again a group of about forty people. When the first lady came in and greeted everyone, she reached out to shake hands with the woman who had met her eight years earlier and addressed her by her name.

The woman who had met her before was astonished. She never expected that the first lady would ever remember her, let alone her name. She was not famous or a large donor. Yet her name was remembered.

What does this tell us? There are two things:

1. The first lady had really good advance people. Obviously she received good briefings before events.

2. It mattered to the first lady to be able to remember names.

With the many people the first lady encountered, recalling names and addressing people specifically would definitely not be expected. Yet obviously that is not what she told herself. She didn't let herself off the hook with an excuse like "I just cannot remember names." Instead, it mattered, and she expected herself to do the best she could and address as many people as possible by name.

> *Remember that a person's name is to that person*
> *the sweetest and most important sound in any language.*
> DALE CARNEGIE

There are many techniques you can use to remember names. Yet none of them matter if remembering doesn't matter to you. What would happen if instead of saying to yourself, "I can't remember names," you simply changed that to "I'm great with names. They matter to me." You would most likely find yourself figuring out how to do it!

YOUR INVISIBLE TOOLBOX

When you meet someone, associating something personal to his or her name will help you better remember it. For example, if someone says to you, "Hello, my name is John," say inwardly to yourself, "John, green eyes like my brother Michael." You have just connected something about John (the color of his eyes) to yourself (your brother has those same green eyes). By associating John with something personal to you, the chances of remembering John's name is greatly increased.

Remember names

15

HOW ARE YOU GUYS COMMUNICATING?

Communications wrought with misunderstanding are nothing new. They happen daily, often very unintentionally. Words spoken can have differing meanings to different ears and minds. Words once used to applaud someone can be spun into indicators of fault when the relationship is threatened.

The single biggest problem with communication is the illusion
that it has taken place.
GEORGE BERNARD SHAW

There are thousands of ways communication can turn out less than positive. Here are three short case studies. The third, being a presidential one, is a reminder that communication mishaps can happen in places where you would imagine the speaker would know better.

Case One: Let me call you Sweetheart...

Has someone ever assumed too much familiarity in their verbal communication with you? Words and the tone they are delivered in have a lot of power, but nothing weakens them more than when they are used inappropriately.

Picture this: You're waiting in the drive-up lane of a new coffee shop. When it's your turn to order your latte, you're greeted with, "What can I get you, hon? Do you want skim in that, hon? Thanks, sweetie, see you at the window." Knowing full well the voice on the other end of the window has never met you and cannot possibly know if you indeed conduct yourself like a sweetie or a hon, you begin to feel a bit uncomfortable. What is this person up to? Is the familiarity supposed to make you feel like a regular here? Do you want to be a regular here? After paying for the latte and hearing two more hons and a bye, sweetie, do you ever want to go back? All you wanted was a latte.

Someone innocently and intentionally was trying to be nice with words and tone. But was that the message received? Or did the speaker unintentionally communicate a message peppered with patronizing words that you received with mild skepticism—making the latte suddenly seeming less desirable?

Case Two: What do you guys think?

Gender issues in the workplace have been examined through news articles, film (recall the classics *Nine to Five* with Dolly Parton or *What Women Want* with Mel Gibson), literature, legal cases, and discussion for years. Exposing these issues has resulted in an attention to gender being formally taken out of the workplace as a consideration in how people are treated. Yet it crops up often in business communication. Have you ever received an e-mail addressed "Gentlemen or Ladies?" They are out there, and in fact they are "out there" in terms of political correctness in today's business environment.

Addressing in a gender-specific way in a written or verbal communication is a thing of the past. Rank and precedence rule in business protocol, not age and/or gender. Yet we still hear, "What do you guys think? Should we ask the ladies? Do the gentlemen care to go to lunch?"

Opening up your language choices to be inclusive, non-gender specific, and free of assumptions creates communication that can reach and be received well by everyone, reflective of the value placed on the receiver's professionalism and your own.

Case Three: The high price of fuel

Even among skilled statesmen, rifts and valleys of unproductive communication can ensue. So it was with US presidents John Adams and Thomas Jefferson. Although friends in their early careers in 1770, by the close of the century they were rivals. Interestingly enough, the rivalry subsided by the end of their lives, and they died close friends once again. Communication added fuel to the rifts and also ended them.

In drafting the Declaration of Independence, Jefferson relied on Adams as a vital contributor. Good communication between the diplomatic Jefferson, who preferred to work behind the scenes, and the self-assured Adams, who was direct in speaking, worked well in fulfilling the goal. Their communications and friendship developed even more as they became diplomats in Europe. Many letters between them proved that they worked well together and appreciated their differences...until their relationship began to strain.

As they began to view the world in differing ways, they started to discredit each other, many times criticizing the very thing in the other they had once applauded. Letters to third parties with negative comments created a decades' long silence and divide, furthered by the unspoken ambition of each man to hold office. Hold office they did, Jefferson following Adams, but the silence between them prevailed until they reached their seventies.

At the age of seventy-five, Adams broke the silence by writing a conciliatory note to Jefferson, and their friendship and communication revived for fifteen years, all the way to July 4, 1826, the day they both died. That day was not only the fiftieth anniversary of the Declaration of Independence but a testament to the power of honest communication. At the end of their lives, Jefferson and Adams were said to have written 158 letters discussing everything they agreed on, not dwelling negatively on the events they held differing views on, and acknowledging where they felt they had been unfair or wrong in their estimation of each other. At the end, their relationship was said to illustrate a clear give and take, with neither man needing to dominate the exchange and with the intent to understand rather than discredit.

One wonders how much more powerful or influential these statesmen might have been had they been able to communicate throughout their lives the way they did at the end. Would they have accomplished even more for themselves and the country they both cared passionately about?

YOUR INVISIBLE TOOLBOX

Do you refer to gender, generation, or use terms that assume familiarity? Do you have any relationships you have let go of due to a communication mishap? You can learn from communications gone wrong. What would the effect be if you addressed people without respect to gender or generation or without communicating assumptions or judgments? What message would be received if you were really careful how you communicated every single time? Think about that one over a latte.

Analyze your communication

16

FRIEND OR FOE

Millennials boasting large social media networks often find themselves with no real friends to hang out with in person. Does this personal situation have implications in the business world?

Yes it does, because there are a variety of reasons to seek to build new relationships in the business world: when identifying prospects for your products or services, reigniting a prior relationship that has drifted, repairing a damaged relationship, or needing to work with a new person who joined your company or your customer's company.

Whenever you meet a new person, either socially or professionally, you automatically ask and answer two questions.

The first question

Friend or foe? Do I like this person? Can I relate to him or her? How similar are we?

When we like someone, we tend to lower our guard and are willing to engage in a conversation—and ultimately in a relationship.

Many of us do business with someone because of a relationship even though factors such as geography or convenience would lead us to a different choice. Hairstylists, accountants, financial planners, pediatricians, veterinarians, tailors are just a few examples of professionals that customers willingly follow to different companies and faraway locations because of a trusted relationship.

Aristotle pointed out this trait of human nature more than 2,300 years ago. He called it "ethos," and his timeless message was that people will do business with people they like, trust, and have confidence in.

Political polls measure likeability of candidates. Customer satisfaction surveys measure the same about organizations. Research shows that the likelihood of a patient filing a malpractice claim against his or her medical provider is linked most closely to the provider's likeability. Numerous studies show that if patients are in good relationships with their doctors there is a strong chance their health will benefit. This holds true even in countries like Japan with distinctly different cultural norms involving communication and relationships.

It is probably no surprise that being liked by your leaders, colleagues, and customers is essential to your career success.

But research also shows that long-lasting success demands more than a good relationship. Relationship-only professionals consistently underperform their highly skilled counterparts in studies. Why?

The second question

This question relates to perceived competence or incompetence. When you meet someone new, you also ask yourself how capable this person is of carrying out his or her intentions toward you (for good or bad). Success in the business world requires that people see you as competent.

When the possible combinations of responses to the friend or foe and competent or incompetent questions are analyzed, people can be quickly assigned to one of four categories.

- Competent friends: These are individuals we relate to and perceive as capable of helping us because we see them as competent. Our trusted vendors, customers, colleagues, friends, mentors, leaders, and family members fall in this category.
- Incompetent friends: These are individuals we like but perceive cannot aid us in the pursuit of our goals because they lack competence. Loved ones we perceive as weak or infirm and the young or elderly often fall in this category. They may be good friends, but we don't call upon them for business guidance because they lack competence in that area.
- Incompetent foes: We don't think much of these individuals and don't worry much about them either. We don't perceive them as capable of harming us because we see them as incompetent. Annoying teenagers, exasperating relatives, addicts causing harm to themselves, and frustrating cashiers fall in this category.
- Competent foes: We don't like these individuals, but we will often play nice because we perceive them as capable of carrying out plans

that may harm us. Competitors in the marketplace, rivals at work, players on opposing sports teams, and those who criticize us or our ideas fall in this category.

A strong foe is better than a weak friend.
EDWARD DAHLBERG

Business referrals and work promotions come from people who see you as competent and likeable. Since many professionals gain a lot of future business from referrals, activities and behaviors that focus on the competent friend category are a good investment of your time and resources.

YOUR INVISIBLE TOOLBOX

Simply building relationships may make for close friendships, but those same people may choose to do business with your competitors because they see you as less capable of helping them with their needs. Your challenge is to build and preserve relationships so people will perceive you as capable and competent in serving them.

Demonstrate your competence

17

THE POWER OF THE WEB

How do you engage with people on a day-to-day basis? Are you texting your best friend while walking down the hallway at work? Are you tracking your favorite sporting event on your device while engaging in conversation at a business event? Are you viewing Facebook posts while standing in line at the bar at a networking function?

The power of the web is not a discussion about the Internet. We're talking about your web of human connections. You already know that most people find new jobs, relationships, and opportunities because of connections through a network. While we all realize the importance of a strong web of network connections, many of us mistakenly think that a large online network is all that's needed. In pursuit of this, we link-in, friend, and follow those we believe can help us and suffer the disappointment when our connections fail to come through.

At the center of the word "networking" is the word "work." It is not enough to merely want a healthy, helpful network. It involves work.

The goal of networking is not only to make more connections but to make a web of connections, many among other people with no obvious link to us. Many people mistakenly think that the network connections closest to them are the ones that are the most important. More commonly, important contacts are made through distant links—people who are not directly connected to us.

To make more distant connections with people who have access to different networks makes for the most effective networking. Relationships must be good so that the links are strong and positive. We can all think of negative links we have with people we've never met thanks to the feedback and word-of-mouth of people within our network.

What's involved in the work of networking? Consider the example of gardeners. Good gardeners carefully till and seed their gardens.

During the growing season, they weed and water them. In the fall they enjoy a bountiful harvest. What happens if gardeners simply threw some seed packets on the ground and didn't care for their gardens? They'd have a bountiful crop of weeds. You can try this over and over again and always get the same results. Do the work, and you'll have a wonderful garden. Just toss some seeds on the ground, and you won't.

The best time to plant a tree was twenty years ago.
The next best time is today.
CHINESE PROVERB

So it is with networking. We can't enjoy the achievement of our goals without doing the work. Like the skilled gardener, the skilled networker knows that the results are not immediate. Yet so many of us think we can harvest a healthy bounty from a network that hasn't been cultivated or cared for. When we are unsuccessful with our approach, we fix blame and complain rather than taking the actions called for.

People who develop the skills of effective networking and do the work required enjoy many benefits. Like the gardener, the benefits are greatly multiplied when the work is done well. The gardener plants only one seed, but each successful seed produces a plant containing hundreds of seeds.

YOUR INVISIBLE TOOLBOX

If you focus more on the people in front of you and less on your devices, you can cultivate the relationships that will ultimately form the critical links that make up your network. Your success depends on it.

Build your network

18

DON'T TALK TO STRANGERS

Millennials typically don't make purchases without first reviewing consumer input. They also tend to rely on testimonials posted by strangers. Because of their heavy trust in user-generated content, millennials are credited for disrupting the rules of commerce.

It is an interesting puzzle that the same people who seek out and trust strangers online to help them make important buying decisions often avoid strangers in the flesh. Hmm.

Contemplate the last conference you attended. Now think about how you entered the room where a session was scheduled to begin. Think about how others entered. How do people choose their seats? Chances are excellent that the seating followed a predictable pattern.

People first look for someone they know to sit with. Locating no familiar faces, most choose to sit alone. Usually they choose a spot along the aisle to allow for a quick exit or at least one seat away from the next person. If that's not an option in a crowded room, they look for someone like themselves (same age, gender, skin color) to sit next to.

A quick glance around most conference rooms reveals that exact pattern. People sitting with colleagues or friends, the seats along the aisles completely filled, and the center sections dotted with individuals seated one, two, or three seats apart.

Don't talk to strangers! This phrase is a common refrain parents and teachers preach to children. It helps keep them safe from predators seeking to harm them by offering candy, pretending to locate a lost pet, or showing false kindness.

As we mature into adulthood, the part of our brain responsible for judgment also matures. We gain the capability to discern which strangers to avoid and which ones we should get to know.

Or do we?

The imprinting in early childhood is so deep that we tend to carry it throughout our lifetimes. As a result, 76 percent of adults suffer from some level of social anxiety. This is the stress that prevents us from forging new relationships with strangers who might be valuable additions to our professional networks and social circles.

Speech has allowed the communication of ideas, enabling human beings to work together to build the impossible. Mankind's greatest achievements have come about by talking, and its greatest failures by not talking. It doesn't have to be like this. Our greatest hopes could become reality in the future. With the technology at our disposal, the possibilities are unbounded. All we need to do is make sure we keep talking.
STEPHEN HAWKING

Does your job require you to interact effectively with people you don't know? Does your career success depend on your ability to forge relationships with strangers?

You are most comfortable when you spend time with people you know and like, but you learn the most when you leave your comfort zone and talk to people you don't know.

YOUR INVISIBLE TOOLBOX

Step out of your comfort zone and take the risk to talk to people you don't regularly interact with. You may be surprised at the creative ideas, innovations, and opportunities you uncover.

Talk to strangers

19

TEND TO YOUR NET

If you want to go fast, go alone. If you want to go far, go with others.
AFRICAN PROVERB

While it is often assumed that the elderly experience loneliness most, it is young people who report feelings of isolation in greater numbers. This may be due to a growing reliance on social technology that leads to quantity over quality in relationships.

The age of social media promotes the illusion that we are creating large networks. While technology allows quick access to information and facilitates speedy communication with people we know, it's a poor substitute for the face-to-face interactions that lead to building strong and lasting relationships.

It is estimated that each of us has a network of 250 people. In support of this theory, if given a little time, you could probably write down the names of 250 people—the people you know on a first name basis. This is the number of people you might invite to your wedding or who might attend your funeral. Experts in networking will tell you how to leverage that network when you need it. They will teach you how to gain access into the networks of others. They will tell you that tapping the networks of others will exponentially increase the size of your own network.

Let's say we list the names of fifty people we know. If each of them knows fifty people and they know fifty people and so on and so on, the numbers add up very quickly. So networking should be fairly simple. Just contact the people we know, tell them what help we need, and voilà, the work of networking is complete.

It isn't that easy. Just because we can list fifty names doesn't mean that we can count on them to help us achieve our goals.

Expert fishermen know to carefully choose their fishing location, select an appropriate lure designed to attract the fish they want, and exercise patience. When they aren't fishing, they're reviewing their successes and failures, watching the weather, planning their next journey, and tending to their nets. They know that their ability to maximize their success rests on the smallest detail—from reviewing their goals to honing their strategy to ensuring the strength of each link in their net. They know it takes time.

So it is with those of us who desire success in our careers. First we attend to the urgent needs of the day, and when we're not actively involved in key activities, we attend to reflection, planning, preparation, and maintenance of the smallest detail.

Or do we?

In our all too busy lives, attending to the work behind the work often doesn't get the attention it deserves. That is, until things don't go as hoped. With a great urgency, we look for shortcuts, we look for efficiency. We look for ease.

What we frequently fail to understand is that if we take the time to strengthen our relationships with others, we are doing more than creating the conditions that will help facilitate career success. We are also creating the environment that leads to enriching personal relationships in the long term.

YOUR INVISIBLE TOOLBOX

Think about the 250 people you know on a first name basis. What can you do to strengthen those relationships?

Tend to your relationships

20

A WASTE OF TIME

Millennials are highly educated, resourceful, team-oriented, and inclusive—at least that's what the prevailing beliefs suggest. They also suggest that millennials are too busy to talk to people, possibly because they're too busy texting friends. Talking to people, especially without a purpose, can seem like a waste of time.

Is it true that millennials don't know how to conduct themselves professionally in the business environment? If so, it's understandable. Most business people haven't received training in etiquette and protocol essential for building and preserving relationships.

Taking time to build a relationship may seem like a time-wasting activity. But building and preserving relationships is important since many of the people you interact with in business will be players in your world for a long time.

Relationship building is not something that only happens in the first few minutes of a meeting during small talk. It's about getting to know the individual as a person, independent of whatever the topic at hand happens to be. Meetings, problems, complaints, compliments, and successes will come and go. The people you work with are often the same people for multiple years.

So, how do you build good relationships?

Skilled hostage negotiators recognize how critical relationship building is. They don't begin their negotiations by making demands and threats. Instead, they build rapport and trust with the hostage-taker. They do this before attempting to negotiate an outcome. If hostage negotiators in high-stakes circumstances and with lives at risk believe they have the time to build relationships, perhaps there's a lesson for us in our jobs.

Have you ever been the irate customer dialing an 800 number to a call center to lodge a complaint? Reflect on how the representative handled your call. When you are addressed in a cordial voice by someone who seems to value you as a person and wants to understand your problem, although still angry, you probably end up using better manners than you would if you were met with a voice on the other end who interrupts you to explain the company's policies on your issue.

Building relationships involves rapport and respect.

> *We don't need to share the same opinions as others,*
> *but we need to be respectful.*
> TAYLOR SWIFT

What if we don't respect the other person? Is it necessary to show respect? Reflect on a hostage scenario, which is clearly a situation with a bilateral lack of respect. The hostage negotiator shows respect anyway. His or her efforts are frequently rewarded in the form of positive outcomes for all concerned.

In our business lives, we should try to build relationships of mutual respect. It doesn't always start that way. It is something we need to work toward over time.

YOUR INVISIBLE TOOLBOX

Respect is an expression of your values. Don't show respect because of who the other person is, show respect because of who you are. Showing respect for others does not reflect weakness. Rather, it conveys strength and confidence. Since people tend to naturally reciprocate, you're more likely to receive respect from others by extending it yourself.

Treat everyone with respect

21

BLAME IT ON GRUMPY CAT

Until one has loved an animal a part of one's soul remains unawakened.
ANATOLE FRANCE

The Internet provides ample evidence that millennials enjoy their pets. Millennials have unseated baby boomers as the largest pet-owning generation.

Millennials welcome four-legged friends into their lives at an average age of twenty-one, considerably younger than their baby boomer elders who waited until age twenty-nine to get their first pet. Whether it is for companionship, a preparatory step for the family they have been delaying, or filling some gap, millennials are taking their pets seriously and pampering them at unprecedented rates.

The world is divided into two different types of people—dog people and cat people.

With over 4.5 billion cat videos posted online, cats are a top pick for millennials. Sixty percent of millennials watch cat videos online, possibly buying into one body of research that says watching cat videos can make you more productive at work. Grumpy Cat (her real name is Tardar Sauce) is perhaps the most famous, and richest, of the Internet felines. Half of millennials own cats, and half of the cat-owning millennials confess to telling their cats secrets that no one else knows.

What about dogs? Millennials are adopting pups at high rates too, with 57 percent of millennial households owning a dog compared with 51 percent of all US households.

While there is strong agreement among millennials about the merits of pet ownership, the segregation between dog people and cat people continues uninterrupted, as it has for generations. We choose our loyalty between dogs and cats much like we choose our favorite sports teams.

And like our favorite teams, we tend to find fault with the opposing team and cheerfully overlook shortcomings on our own side.

Dog people commonly hold negative impressions of cats, such as cats only care about themselves, are loners, are cold and unfeeling, and black cats bring bad luck.

Not to be outdone, cat people hold their own negative perceptions of dogs, usually vilifying them by breed rather than amassing all dogs into a single cohort.

Whatever our bias, dogs or cats, we acquired it as a result of the knowledge and experiences we've had. Biases and stereotypes are normal. We all have them. We hold biases about pets, people, members of a certain generation, careers, our business competition, industries, products, beliefs…about almost everything. As we expand our knowledge and broaden our experiences, we naturally challenge our biases and stereotypes—usually with good outcomes.

The more you are open to learning about a wide range of things, people, and experiences, especially those unfamiliar to you, the more your potential has a chance to fully mature and your own life is enriched.

YOUR INVISIBLE TOOLBOX

One of your greatest challenges is to ensure that your biases, either conscious or unconscious ones, don't hold you back or prevent you from reaching your potential.

Challenge your biases

22

IN THE HEAT OF CONFLICT

When you grow up with texting as a primary method of communication, where and how do you develop interpersonal and conflict resolution skills? It's possible that you don't. Lacking the volume of phone and face-to-face experiences of previous generations, you may even struggle to accurately decode the nonverbal elements of communication that aren't present when communicating is one-sided, brief, and electronic. You may even misinterpret disagreement as yelling—a misunderstanding at the heart of many cross-generational conflicts.

For good ideas and true innovation, you need human interaction,
conflict, argument, debate.
MARGARET HEFFERNAN

Say a colleague takes credit for your idea. A manager sets an unrealistic deadline. A family member doesn't perform the household chores as agreed. Your inability to stick with your diet and exercise program is frustrating. Conflict takes many forms. And whether it's with a coworker, manager, loved one, or self, conflict takes a heavy toll on relationships and productivity.

The ability to deal well with conflict is a rare skill. Hardwired at birth for fight or flight, we default to aggressive or passive behaviors that produce only losers and no winners. Is there another way?

The single biggest thing that characterizes conflict is heightened emotions. How can you manage your own emotions in the heat of a conflict? Here are two tips:

1. Find something to occupy your mind and distract you. Physical activity is always a good choice. Avoid activities that allow you to ruminate (e.g., driving or shopping) as you are unlikely to cool down and may get more worked up.

2. If you can't physically leave the environment, consciously change your emotional state. Silently say the alphabet or your social security number backward. Try counting backward from 1,000 by 3s. It's difficult to remain emotional when your mind is challenged with such a complex task.

YOUR INVISIBLE TOOLBOX

Conflict, when done well, is an important and inevitable part of progress. When you experience conflict, you must challenge yourself to shift your emotional state. With a cooler head, you'll be ready to address the conflict, challenge your assumptions, and recognize that your evaluation of the situation is probably only one of several interpretations.

Shift your emotional state

23

VARIETY IS THE SPICE OF LIFE

It is time for parents to teach young people early on
that in diversity there is beauty and there is strength.
MAYA ANGELOU

One of the most endearing qualities about millennials is their inclusiveness. Millennials, it's said, are the most accepting generation to date when it comes to diversity.

When we think about diversity, we often consider only visible diversity. Things like race, gender, age, and physical challenges.

Just as there are many invisible tools that have a profound impact in organizations, there are many invisible aspects to diversity that are often overlooked, probably because we can't see them, and they seem hidden.

A team can be made up of members who are visibly diverse, but if their thinking approaches are similar, the full benefits of meaningful diversity are not available to that team.

There is wide-sweeping agreement that high-performing teams are made up of individuals who are focused on common goals, share common values, and agree on a common vision.

What is less understood (and often misunderstood) are the ways in which members of high-performing teams interact. Many teams are labeled as high-performing because they come to quick agreement on decisions, seem to be in sync with each other, and speak with a common voice. A more careful analysis often reveals that those team characteristics are actually evidence of a team suffering from sameness—a serious lack of diversity in thinking, viewpoints, and approaches.

YOUR INVISIBLE TOOLBOX

High-performing teams, if they are truly comprised of both visible and invisible diversity, will take longer to make decisions, will experience greater conflict, and will produce results that any subset of the group could not have delivered independently.

Seek invisible diversity

24

THE DANGERS OF STEREOTYPING

When you think about the baby boomer generation, what comes to mind? Competitive? Live to work? Loyal to employers? Ambitious? Politically correct? Strong work ethic? Goal-centric? Disciplined?

There is an excellent chance that the things that come to your mind when you think of baby boomers are an incomplete and inaccurate stereotype of an entire generation and the individuals born into it. The same is true of the stereotypes ascribed to millennials.

Each of us is, mostly unconsciously, programmed with filters that lead to the stereotypes we hold. Our family of origin largely influences our programming, especially early in life. For better or worse, our beliefs about money, race, gender, age, religion, politics, the environment, and so on are often shared among family members as if they were encoded in our DNA. Our cultural programming causes us to look at the world through the lens of that culture. Our education system imprints us with filters. Our peer groups influence the way we view the world. Our leaders indoctrinate us into a corporate culture.

The media plays a role in shaping the stereotypes we hold. Our loyalties to our favorite sports teams and aversion to others are so deep, it's as if they were tattooed on us at birth. Our past experiences color our future experiences.

Do the stereotypes that emerge because of our filters help us or harm us? That's an important question for all of us to ponder.

A stereotype may be negative or positive, but even positive stereotypes present two problems: They are clichés, and they present a human being as far more simple and uniform than any human being actually is.
NANCY KRESS

Consider several commonly held negative stereotypes about millennials and think about how these filters may lead to negative consequences in the workplace.

- They are self-centered and entitled.
- They are attached to their devices.
- They expect a trophy just for showing up.
- They have been overindulged by their parents.
- They are stimulus junkies.

Even positive labels can have negative unintended consequences. Here are some common examples of positive filters people hold of millennials. When these stereotypes exist, we may be missing opportunities.

- They are techno savvy.
- They are team players.
- They are diversity focused.
- They are open to new ideas.
- They want to please others.

YOUR INVISIBLE TOOLBOX

What are some of the interactions you've had with others that were impacted by stereotypes? What are some of the stereotypes you hold? Are they helping or hurting?

Challenge stereotypes

25

ARE THINGS REALLY WHAT THEY SEEM?

Millennials have heard it all. They are entitled, tech savvy, value driven. The list goes on and on. Some of these evaluations might flatter them, others might make them angry. Is it fair?

If you ask people if they stereotype, most would answer no. Stereotyping typically insinuates a less than fair appraisal of a person or group, oftentimes linked to a negative prejudice. Most of us would not want to affirm that we stereotype because of this definition. As a member of some classification or other throughout the course of our lives we realize at least a bit of what it feels like to be categorized rather than seen as an individual. It does not feel good or just.

Is stereotyping always negative?

Stereotyping was first defined by journalist Walter Lippman in 1922. Lippman referred to stereotypes early on as pictures in our heads. He defined stereotyping as a selection process that organizes and simplifies perceptions of others, forming the mental representation that's then held of them. Lippman felt stereotypes created expectations regarding how people of various groups behaved, and as humans we unconsciously seek to confirm those expectations when communicating.

Why have these preformed expectations of the mind become so undesirable when obviously the process is natural?

It is because in our interpersonal interactions with someone different than ourselves, we often allow the stereotype to dictate what we experience (or even if we will experience) rather than allowing it to be our first best guess, willing to adjust it based on our interaction.

As Lippman asserted, in communicating, humans tend to process information more readily that is consistent with their preformed mental model. This unconscious stereotyping can directly influence how effectively we initially get to know people. We run the risk of assuming what may not be entirely true, as well as not fully recognizing or seeing the actual similarities or differences present.

Stereotyping as a function of the mind will never go away. In fact, you wouldn't want it to. It's a sign that you recognize differences do exist rather than being blind to them or assuming false similarity and familiarity. The negative connotation and risk associated with them, however, can be eliminated if you do the following three things.

1. Become conscious and aware of the stereotypes you currently hold. What factual information can you add to what you know to increase the reliability of what you think?

2. Be flexible. Check your interactions against the preformed stereotype. Stay open to changing thought based on actual experience.

3. Monitor your thinking so you are describing rather than evaluating. Be aware not to assign value to difference. Simply describe the differences that exist. Staying descriptive prevents prejudices cropping up.

When you consciously use and manage stereotypes, they become an initial tool in interpersonal, transgenerational, and cross-cultural communication. They can provide you with a platform to begin collecting real-time understandings of others who are different from you.

Then if someone asks you, "Do you stereotype?" you can answer, "Yes, and effectively."

Stereotypes lose their power when the world is found to be more complex than the stereotype would suggest. When we learn that individuals do not fit the group stereotype, then it begins to fall apart.
ED KOCH

You should feel good that by initially stereotyping, you're not being culturally blind. Rather, you're recognizing that differences do exist. You can demonstrate that you're willing and able to suspend evaluating people based on expectation and embrace the experience of being fully open when getting to know others who are different.

YOUR INVISIBLE TOOLBOX

Which groups of people have you formed stereotypes of? Choose to describe the differences rather than evaluate the differences.

Describe differences

26

YOU HAVE A CHOICE OF AIRLINES

Millennials are assumed to possess strong technological skills. Is that true? It's also assumed that they have proficiency in one or more of the hard skills such as math, science, engineering, and the like. Is that an accurate description of your workplace strengths? Further, it has been suggested that millennials were raised to believe that hard skills matter most when it comes to success. Do you agree with that view?

On the other hand, it's also widely accepted that millennials lack soft skills and social graces, especially communication in the workplace. Is that true?

Whether favoritism to hard skills over soft skills is an accurate generalization of an entire generation or simply true of some individuals is a minor point. The major point is the critical importance of both hard and soft skills to career and organizational success. When one is lacking, there's a wide opening for failure to occur.

Imagine you are jetting through the friendly skies. Your pilot has just announced that you have arrived at your cruising altitude of 31,000 feet. Do you trust that the pilot and crew possess the technical skills to handle whatever situation they may encounter? At this point, you have little choice.

It's interesting that you've placed complete trust in someone you've never met, will probably never meet, and only hear speak a couple of sentences. You blindly trust that the captain and crew of your chosen airline are technically capable. Confident in this, you return to your technology and think only fleetingly about the content of the safety briefing that is part of the welcome aboard routine on every flight.

Is it your good fortune to be flying on the airline that employs the most technically capable people? That's doubtful. You must assume the crews of all major airlines possess similar technical skill.

You have a choice of airlines as your flight attendants will remind you in the next hour when they repeat the phrase that they must say in their sleep by now: *"We know you have a choice of airlines, and we thank you for choosing to fly with us. When your plans call for air travel in the future, we hope to see you again on one of our flights."*

Yes, you do have a choice. How do you choose?

Most of us begin by looking to our immediate short-term interests—the flight schedules and cost. This usually narrows the choices to two or three possibilities. How do we choose from the short list? We choose based on who we think will treat us the best. That's why airline loyalty programs are so popular. They provide us with some sense of comfort that we will receive preferential treatment and service during our travel experience.

That same process is how most of us make the decision about who we will do business with.

We see our customers as invited guests to a party, and we are the hosts.
It's our job to make the customer experience a little bit better.
JEFF BEZOS

Research supports this statement. According to Harvard University, Stanford Institute, and the Carnegie Foundation, only 15 percent of success is due to technical skills. In most industries, the people we serve assume a level of technical capability. It is the people skills that are the differentiator, to the tune of 85 percent.

If your flight experience was satisfactory, you will likely include this airline in your future travel plans—unless and until another airline figures out how to leverage the 85 percent of their success that relies on the people skills that take customer experiences to a new level.

Across almost every industry—air travel, hospitality, healthcare, financial services, retail, and so on—process and technical abilities are fairly easy to copy. The competitive advantage goes to those who treat the people they serve the best. Even when transactions are conducted business-to-business rather than business-to-consumer, it is important to realize that people are always at the center of decision-making.

YOUR INVISIBLE TOOLBOX

Businesses don't do business with businesses, people do business with people. And people want to be treated well.

Enrich the personal experience

27

#WINNING

"Half of millennials have said 'People my age see real life as a video game' and almost 6 out of 10 said '#winning is the slogan of my generation.' Certainly #epicfail seems to have become their anti-slogan!"

"To anyone who has spent as much time with millennials as we at MTV have (and certainly for anyone who employs as many millennials as we do), it quickly becomes apparent how adept this generation is at navigating the loopholes, trap doors, and 'Easter eggs' of life using their smarts, technological resources, and 'peer power.'"

In the *Harvard Business Review* article entitled "Millennials Are Playing with You," Nick Shore made these observations.

Shore goes on to say that millennials tend to demand fairness, transparency, and clear rules. If this is the case, your generation seems primed to value solving problems in a mutually beneficial way.

Tougher to achieve when working through an issue with a person versus a program or game, your route to making a decision or solving problems requires a consciousness around strategies when working interpersonally.

Compromise was once thought to be the best result we could get for any problem or decision involving differing positions. Fifty/fifty for each party made sense and still does. But just like in gaming, isn't it always best for everyone to strive for more?

When solving a problem or making a decision, human nature prompts us to go straight to solution. Although this appeals to a sense of efficiency, it shortchanges us more often than not.

If your grandmother died and left a diamond ring to you and your sibling and you both wanted it, how would you determine who gets it? You might discuss sharing it, dividing the time you use it equally. That's an option. You might consider taking out the stone, giving one of you the stone and the other the gold setting. That's an option. You might state your position that you should have it (because you are older or were closer to Grandma). That's an option.

In the process of going straight to options, you might notice some unproductive emotions, as you may both have reasons for wanting the ring, and the options and discussion don't include how you feel. So a compromise might be settled on, but in the long term, can you be sure it feels right to both of you? Was it the best you could do? #Epicfail.

The ability to go beyond compromise depends on two things:

1. Recognizing in any situation that you need to have a continual focus on maintaining the relationship, as well as clarifying what you're trying to solve.

2. Asking why before going to options. You both have interests in the ring. What are they? Why is the ring important? What does it mean to each of you? Sharing the "why" allows you to find out more about each other. This leads to a better relationship and more options.

Collaboration is a result that can only be achieved through refraining from going straight to compromise. Time spent nurturing the relationship, being soft on the person and hard on the issue, matters. Exploring the whys of positions brought to the table before designating options pays dividends. In the case of the ring, you might find out underlying reasons each of you have that will guide you to much more than a 50/50 solution.

"Positive randomness" is a gaming technique that resonates with millennials. Shore says, "If a game is too predictable, it is boring, but if there are too many random surprises, it is too complex. The perfect combination is enough structure to understand the rules, with enough unpredictability to keep it interesting in perpetuity."

In moving from compromise to collaboration, focusing first on the relationship, the goal, and the underlying interest gives you a structure to govern the game of solving problems and making decisions, as well as an essence of positive randomness as you explore and discover interests. In the next problem you solve with someone, ask why that person has taken the position he or she has.

YOUR INVISIBLE TOOLBOX

Explore taking a decision from a compromise to collaboration. Rather than a predictable 50/50, you'll achieve a more interesting and mutually beneficial result. You create more possibility in order to come away with a greater #win.

Ask why

28

THERE IS NO "I" IN "TEAM"

Unlike previous generations who grew up in organizations with large corporate hierarchies and a focus on individual contribution, millennials favor teamwork and team-based roles. Millennials have also met the dark side of teams when the lion's share of the work for a team school project or team work assignment fell to only one or two members of the team. How can these contradictions be reconciled?

We don't have to look far to find proof of the stunning success of teams within organizations. Teams are one of the most effective responses to today's business challenges—challenges posed by customer service, quality, continuous improvement, and all the other hot topics that separate today's market winners from the companies they leave in the dust.

In pursuit of this competitive advantage, leaders commonly remind employees that there is no "I" in "Team." "We" becomes the mantra.

Beware! There are risks. The word "we" means nothing to you. It means nothing to any of us.

For organizations to be successful, each individual must see him or herself as accountable for a final result. Even in the case of team goals, each individual must understand and carry out his or her specific role and responsibilities. Giving up accountability to "the team" sends a powerful message to our subconscious minds to look for excuses rather than to take actions that will move us closer to the goal.

Accountability breeds response-ability.
STEPHEN COVEY

Most sports teams imprint the goal of "we will win." The most successful sports teams know that they can't stop there. They take it one step further by having each individual member of the team imprint the specific role he or she is accountable for as part of the team goal.

Consider this familiar example. Why does one parent sleep through a baby's cry in the middle of the night while the other parent needs only to hear a change in the breathing of the child to be on red alert?

When parents bring their newborn baby home, both are on heightened alert for anything that may represent a threat to the infant. After a few days pass, the task typically falls to one parent who most consistently rushes to the child's side at the slightest peep.

The other parent remains in deep sleep. Imagine the surprise of the well-rested parent who discovers in the morning that his or her cranky, sleep-deprived partner was up five times during the night with the child.

None of us realize that we block sounds from our peaceful sleep every night (furnace or air conditioner coming on, TV set blaring, music from next door, sirens down the street). We don't hear the many sounds that occur in our homes every night.

Why does one parent block the baby's cry and the other doesn't? Isn't the baby valuable to both of them?

Of course the child is important to both parents. It isn't a question of buying into the value of the new life. It's because one parent has given up accountability. One parent knows the other will get up, allowing his or her subconscious to rest soundly in the knowledge that "the parenting team" has it handled.

A similar phenomenon happens in the workplace. Every team has one or two individual(s) who everyone knows "she will" or "he will." The comfort of that knowledge allows other members of the team to rest their creativity, their talents, and their awareness.

Giving up accountability causes us to miss a lot of opportunities and warning signs that will take us more speedily to the achievement of our goals. To be fully accountable means we need to know what is expected of us. In this way, we engage both our conscious and subconscious creative genius.

YOUR INVISIBLE TOOLBOX

There may not be an "I" in "Team," but teams are made up of individuals, and each individual needs to be accountable for his or her role, responsibilities, and expectations.

Be fully accountable

Part II

TOOLS FOR PRESENTING YOURSELF IN THE WORLD

How do you want to be perceived?

You present yourself all day, every day. You show up to the workplace, in meetings, and at events. The impression you make on others happens both verbally and nonverbally. Presenting yourself effectively, whether one-on-one or to groups, ranks high on the lists of qualities identified for success in the workplace. Yet in spite of the strong awareness most people seem to have for the importance of these skills, they don't maximize the impact they make in day-to-day interactions.

As technology advances and becomes easier to use, people often find face-to-face interactions more difficult. As a result, presentations fail, opportunities are lost, relationships suffer, and business results fall short of goals.

In a business environment that has never been more competitive, research shows that success depends about six times more on our ability to present ourselves effectively than it does on technical skills.

In this part of the book, we examine the tools for presenting ourselves effectively.

Trust yourself. Create the kind of self that you will be happy to live with all your life. Make the most of yourself by fanning the tiny inner sparks of possibility into flames of achievement.
GOLDA MEIR

29

CAUGHT ON CAMERA

What threats did your parents make to pressure or coerce you into good behavior?

Members of previous generations were cautioned to consider what their mothers or grandmothers would think of their actions if they were headlined on the front page of the local newspaper. This warning gave pause for many and often nudged them into making different behavioral choices. The idea of embarrassing stories playing out in the daily newspapers kept the threat credible.

For millennials, the imaginary wagging finger of the parent or shaming from the grandparent has been replaced by very real and watchful electronic eyes. They're cameras and drones. They're everywhere. They're effective. Information Handling Services, based in London, UK, estimated that there were 245 million professionally installed video surveillance cameras operating globally in 2014. The numbers will only increase in the years ahead.

That doesn't even account for the new wave of body cameras worn by police officers across the United States or the staggering number of recording devices carried by private individuals.

Don't worry that children never listen to you; worry that
they are always watching you.
ROBERT FULGHUM

Carlesha Freeland-Gaither was twenty-two years old and a nursing assistant. In November 2014, a surveillance camera caught a man abducting her and forcing her into an old Ford Taurus in Philadelphia. Freeland-Gaither's impressive fight, including kicking out the windows of the car, was also captured by the camera.

Philadelphia police released the video to the public, where it attracted national media attention and prompted a team of detectives in Virginia to show the footage to the father of a violent offender they were searching for. When the father identified the car as belonging to his son, another technology was tapped.

The car had been outfitted with GPS by the local car dealership that used the controversial practice to track cars sold to owners with bad credit. The GPS led police to a parking lot in Maryland where the perpetrator surrendered and an injured Freeland-Gaither was rescued. Thanks to technology linking activities across three states, Delvin Barnes was arrested and Carlesha Freeland-Gaither was returned to her family.

From the arrest of Delvin Barnes to the identification of the Boston Marathon bombing suspects through grainy security camera images to the embarrassing releases of audio and video recordings cutting short numerous business and political careers, there is mounting evidence that our behaviors are being constantly monitored.

Behaviors clearly improve when cameras roll, resulting in drops in both crimes and poor choices. There is more on the horizon. Facial-recognition software is making sifting through mountains of footage much easier. This is good news for crime fighters and bad news for individuals inclined to bad behavior. More advanced technologies are not far behind.

What does all this recording mean for millennials?

YOUR INVISIBLE TOOLBOX

Thanks to surveillance cameras, behaviors are on display all day every day in public settings. The continuous monitoring of public and nonpublic venues may be a target of privacy advocates, but it's hard to argue with the results.

Act like you're being watched

30

THE ONLY MESSAGE THAT MATTERS

Millennials are often cited as being socially awkward. The technology they excel in may have left a deficit in the demonstrations of their behaviors as a person. HBO host, comedian, and cultural critic Bill Maher said it this way: "This is a generation who has lived their entire lives through a screen." Sound a bit unfair? This observation might apply to more than your generation.

A recent employee engagement survey conducted by an organization's human resources department revealed a significant trust deficit between employees and their senior leaders. To analyze the situation and get to the bottom of it, a consulting group was brought in.

Expecting to hear sordid details of breaches of trust in the final report, the CEO couldn't believe his ears when he discovered that the focus of much of the feedback from the consulting group applied to him and the message he was communicating in the hallway—a message of being unapproachable and disinterested in his employees.

Needless to say, that was not his intention. He was part of the second generation running this successful family-owned company, and he loved and sincerely valued all the employees. In many respects, this company was his family.

What did the report highlight as the crime he was guilty of perpetrating to cause this kind of feedback? The employees reported his attention was focused on his handheld device whenever he walked down the hall. The technology received the benefits of his eye contact rather than him using his eye contact to nonverbally greet employees as he passed them in the halls. The message was surprising. The message was powerful.

There are managers so preoccupied with their e-mail messages that they never look up from their screens to see what's happening in the non-digital world.
MIHALY CSIKSZENTMIHALYI

This was something he could consciously change.

In today's world, with today's technology, eye contact with devices is more prevalent than eye contact with people. The message this sends can be destructive: "I have more important things to attend to than you." In contrast, by resisting the temptation to look at your device, you're communicating respect and value to others.

There's a reason hitchhikers and charity bell ringers use eye contact. They have proof based on donations and rides that it will get attention and instill trust. Walking down the hall was an opportunity for the CEO to build trust simply by looking at people.

The idea of focusing on those around us in order to communicate that we value them may sound simple. Yet it's not easy to do in actuality. Have you ever been talking with someone at an event and he or she was looking over your shoulder to see who else might be coming into the room? The message received screams louder than anything that person may be saying.

It doesn't matter what you meant to say. It doesn't even matter what you actually did say. The only message that matters is the one received. If others come away from interacting with you believing you're confident, interesting, interested, and knowledgeable, you have achieved a successful outcome in communication. If they feel you're insincere, uninformed, or disingenuous, it doesn't matter that you're credible, confident, and that your message is reliable, the damage is done. A message was received.

YOUR INVISIBLE TOOLBOX

What percent of your attention is distracted by or goes to a device rather than those around you?

Monitor your device time

31

THE WHITE HOUSE CRASHERS

On a crisp November evening in 2009, more than three hundred guests, including celebrities, were gathered for a White House dinner in honor of visiting Indian Prime Minister Manmohan Singh.

Among the guests was a woman dressed in a red sari, accompanied by her husband, attired in a black tuxedo. Although uninvited, they made their way through the crowd as if they were supposed to be there. They passed through several security points, each guard reporting that "they looked as if they belonged." They met President Barack Obama and rubbed shoulders with Vice President Joe Biden before someone realized they were crashing the party.

These two individuals will forever be known as the White House Crashers. How did Michaela and Tareq Salahi crash a White House party?

Dr. Albert Mehrabian, professor and researcher at the University of California at Los Angeles (UCLA), showed that 55 percent of the impact we have on others comes from the visual elements of communication such as body language, eye contact, attire, and facial expression. Thirty-eight percent of the impact in face-to-face communication comes from vocal quality, things like intonation, speed, and clarity, while the remaining 7 percent comes from the words used.

When the guards said the Salahis looked like they belonged, this provides evidence to support Mehrabian's research study.

They expect a professional presentation, so they expect to see a professional. Dress appropriately for the occasion, but don't be one of the crowd.
WESS ROBERTS

Frank Abagnale is perhaps the most famous con artist of modern times. His resume includes check forger ($2.5 million worth of forged checks across twenty-six countries) and impostor (he claims to have been an airline pilot, doctor, US Bureau of Prisons agent, and lawyer, among other professions). His story served as the inspiration for an autobiography, a Broadway musical, and a motion picture all titled *Catch Me If You Can*. How was Abagnale able to con so many people?

One of the influential factors in forming perceptions involves the regard for authority. A title or uniform automatically evokes authority, commanding respect and compelling people to follow the leadership of the person with the title or uniform.

Frank Abagnale knew exactly what uniform to don to get the results he sought.

What has this got to do with you?

Dr. Robert Cialdini, social psychologist and author of *Influence – The Psychology of Persuasion*, contends that in the corporate world, a business suit can be considered a uniform of authority. In one study, he reports that pedestrians followed a man jaywalking in a business suit, but not when the same man jaywalked in casual attire.

Does this mean that wearing a business suit, or in the case of the White House crashers, formal attire is the only option if you want to establish favorable perceptions? Certainly not.

Individuals and organizations need to determine what "uniform" is appropriate and effective to communicate to both the internal and external audience the values and goals they embrace. A uniform is more than an outfit. Your websites, e-mails, social media presence are all factors that help determine how people view you. There has to be congruency.

Because we tend to believe what we see, even a long-lasting reputation can be compromised if what people see in person doesn't match the ideal of the person they have formulated in their minds.

YOUR INVISIBLE TOOLBOX

What two words do you want people to think of when they think of you professionally? Does your attire and image across all platforms communicate those words?

Determine your desired image

32

LOOK ME IN THE EYES

Once upon a time, I took a Landmark Education class, in which we were told to silently hold eye contact with a stranger for 5 minutes. I did the exercise twice. Once, I was paired with a woman 25 years older, and by the end of the exercise, I wanted to kiss her. Why? Probably because the only people I've ever looked at for that long are people I've kissed.

The next time, I was paired with a guy. The beginning felt like a boxing stare down—the other man gazing coolly into my eyes as if itching for a fight. I couldn't help but to smile at how he was trying to exude toughness in an exercise designed to foster intimacy. Thankfully, by the end of 5 minutes, no punches were exchanged (no kisses either), but we did feel artificially close, even without exchanging any words.

EVAN MARC KATZ

For millennials to be persuaded, it is said, they must experience things first.

Have you ever said to someone, "Look me in the eyes and say that!"? We all have. Why do we do this? We do it because we tend to trust people who look us in the eyes. In fact, it is this tool that allows people of low integrity to persuade others to believe that they are honest and sincere.

Eye contact is one of the most intimate forms of communication. The recipient of your gaze feels more connected and positive toward you. Eye contact sends messages even when words aren't exchanged. It communicates interest or hostility, value or indifference, empathy or triviality, dominance or submissiveness, agreement or defiance, appreciation or anger.

A lot of meanings are communicated with eye contact. It can signal the start of building a trusting relationship or the start of a fight. Most of us take eye contact for granted and don't regard it as a tool or communication skill worthy of dedicating time to master.

An animal's eyes have the power to speak a great language.
MARTIN BUBER

Eye contact is also an important tool in the messages we receive. We may think that listening is a task left to our ears, but in face-to-face communication, eye contact communicates listening more than anything else.

If you've communicated with someone across a room without exchanging a single word, you already know the power of eyes in sending messages. Why don't we translate this appreciation for the power of eye contact into action?

It isn't easy.

Looking at others can make us feel vulnerable or insecure. We know that eye contact makes an interaction more intimate. We avoid eye contact with people we don't like or if we're trying to hide the truth from someone. Masking our emotions is more easily done when we avoid eye contact. If we're concerned about how our message may be received by someone, we may avoid eye contact to avoid the discomfort.

Eye contact is important because people are social creatures. You may be surprised to discover that you aren't making eye contact nearly as much as you thought you were.

YOUR INVISIBLE TOOLBOX

Looking people in the eye and holding their gaze can help to persuade, relate, win over, and connect with others. If you employ eye contact when communicating, you allow others to experience you and your ideas.

Increase your eye contact

—————————————— 33 ——————————————

DON'T ASSUME A FIG

What you do speaks so loud that I cannot hear what you say.
RALPH WALDO EMERSON

It is to their advantage for millennials to develop a blended communication approach of high tech and high touch. Although face-to-face interactions might at first seem archaic when so much can be determined by a few thumb flicks on a device, recognizing how to leverage these interactions is an opportunity to positively differentiate both yourself and the interaction. With the emphasis on collaborative work spaces and the death of the singular cubicle, millennials have daily opportunity to be seen and to interact.

If there were a way you could instill trust immediately, boost people's perceptions of your confidence and competence that cost you nothing and could be employed whenever you choose, would you be interested?

One branch of neuro-linguistic programming (NLP) is the study of the messages body language sends. We message people without saying a word. NLP has proven humans trust symmetry. We look for and trust symmetry. Conversely, we tend to distrust imbalance.

It's in your best interest to seek to communicate trust and sincerity, and symmetrical body language supports this goal.

Symmetrical posture that triggers trust is a balanced stance with your arms at your sides. Can you gesture? Absolutely. Just drop your arms after the gesture to create a neutral symmetrical appearance.

Since this stance isn't comfortable or natural, your body doesn't naturally fall into symmetrical poses. Most interactions that involve others create a bit of tension. Adrenaline pumps through the body, and as a result, you tend to posture yourself in ways that make you comfortable or cover and protect your most vulnerable areas.

Have you seen the fig leaf pose? This is a classic where people cross their hands in front of their lower belly or crotch. Those assuming "the fig" feel more comfort in this pose. Unfortunately, that's not the message they send. The fig communicates weakness.

Have you ever seen an actor on the red carpet in the fig? It is rare. Actors know they "sell" themselves or the idea of who they are at those events. It's not just the designer outfit that's important to create the image they're after. Their posture communicates confidence and surety. Do you really think they feel confident and sure inside right before they compete for an award and enter a room of incredibly talented people from their own industry? Probably not. So they let their posture take the lead and do the job for them.

Another comfort pose is crossing your arms and protecting your core or your heart. It is comfortable (especially if you're cold) and protective. Is it effective in the message? No. It closes you off, creates a psychological barrier between you and those you're talking to, and doesn't give you any chance to gesture and enhance your presence.

We may not be actors selling a persona, but we are "selling" our expertise each day. Our ideas, our competency, and whether or not we can be trusted are all negotiable based on how we appear. Body language can predict the outcome of interactions such as job interviews, dating, and negotiations with an average accuracy of 80 percent, according to an MIT study by Dr. Alex Pentland. It is best to have it communicate well for us.

YOUR INVISIBLE TOOLBOX

Open your posture by standing with your arms at your sides. Monitor how you feel. Uncomfortable? Strike an "open posture pose" every chance you get and challenge yourself to move past your comfort in order to communicate trust and confidence.

Open your posture

34

WHO SMILED FIRST?

With less and less opportunity for face-to-face interactions due to remote work spaces and technology, the interactions we do have with others are extremely important. Yet with the reality of less interaction, the habits of monitoring how we appear during our interactions become lax. Much like our bodies when we don't exercise, the expressions and features of our faces become sedentary if not prompted by use in face-to-face interactions.

It's said that the most important thing you wear is the expression on your face.

Most of us are unaware of the message our facial expressions communicate to those around us. This is especially true when we find ourselves in a stressful setting such as when we're asked to speak to a group of people or chair a meeting.

It is known that smiling boosts our immune system, which helps us relax in tough situations. Smiling also lowers our blood pressure and releases endorphins and serotonin. A smile also humanizes us and our message. More than 30 percent of us smile more than twenty times a day, and less than 14 percent of us smile less than five times a day. Children smile four hundred times a day on average. We also know from research experiments where people are shown faces that those with happy expressions are more memorable. Don't we all want to be memorable?

A warm smile is the universal language of kindness.
WILLIAM ARTHUR WARD

What if the message you're delivering is a serious one? It will be difficult to emphasize serious points if you maintain a serious facial expression throughout. Varying your facial expression to match your message and challenging yourself to smile more often will make you more effective.

Have you ever noticed that you respond with a smile when someone smiles at you? Try this experiment. The next time you're a customer, try smiling at your service provider. It doesn't matter if he or she is a waiter, flight attendant, TSA agent, consultant, clerk, accountant, or any other profession, the results are the same. You can impact how the other person responds with your actions.

Become conscious of the power of a smile. How often are you smiling in a given day?

YOUR INVISIBLE TOOLBOX

What can you elicit from others by initiating a smile? How do you condition yourself to be the one who initiates the smile? There is so much to be gained.

Initiate a smile

35

WALK LIKE A MODEL

Who are the power millennials? Who are the millennials who have made the biggest difference in the world so far? The list is impressive and growing. Here are just a few:

Mark Zuckerberg is responsible for Facebook, the social media platform used by about 25 percent of the world's population to document their lives and interests. Justin Bieber holds the record for the most songs in the Billboard Hot 100 chart and has shattered records held by the Beatles. Beyoncé is the highest-ranked millennial on the Forbes list of the one hundred most powerful women. Lady Gaga is a songwriter, singer, actress, dancer, and fashion designer also well respected for championing the rights of people less able to speak for themselves.

For most members of the millennial generation, the enormous wealth, fame, and good works that characterize those named on the list above are still elusive. For them, some power lessons from the runway might be useful.

We're not talking about the runway at the airport. We're talking about the fashion runway or catwalk.

How does a model carry him or herself on the runway? Tero's research on communication has roots in the modeling world and even today extends far beyond academic studies. Preparing contestants for the Miss America Pageant has more in common with preparing business leaders for success on the stage than most people realize.

Showing up is essential. Showing up consistently is powerful.
Showing up consistently with a positive outlook is even more powerful.
JEFF OLSON

What are the commonalities?

Whether in a boardroom or on the catwalk, people communicate power when they take up space. Open, expansive stances communicate confidence and power when they are seated in a meeting or standing on a platform. When making an entrance, whether walking that runway at a fashion show or entering the door of a networking function, a powerful posture and walk is one that takes up space. Elongating your frame, taking long strides, keeping your shoulders back, and swinging your arms confidently serves to alert people around you that you are confident and powerful (even if you don't feel that way).

Your physical presence shapes the perceptions people hold of you, which can help shape your success in business.

YOUR INVISIBLE TOOLBOX

Choose body postures and movement that communicate power and confidence. It's one of the simplest nonverbal things you can do to further your career.

Make an entrance

36

GIVE IT TO ME QUICK

Presence is more than just being there.
MALCOLM FORBES

Millennials are used to information coming at them from every direction and quickly. They filter out what isn't needed and use what is. But developing professional presence with all this stimulus takes time.

How do you handle all your life demands and come off with a professional presence that exudes the message that you have everything under control? Dorothea Johnson, founder of the Protocol School of Washington, DC, has wise advice on how to appear professional. "In business, never run! Carry yourself elegantly to be perceived as competent."

How do you look when the many competing events of the day make you so time conscious that you physically run, not walk, from obligation to obligation? What message do you send when you run? Certainly not one of confident professionalism.

Think about it. Talking too fast and too much is the equivalent to running. Acting without thinking calmly first, giving others abrupt responses, finishing others' sentences, and physically appearing rushed can all give the message that you're having trouble handling what's on your plate.

To maintain professionalism, never let them see you sweat. How can you avoid that? Work consciously on open receptive body posture and a calm facial expression and vocal tone. Carry yourself with gracious confidence, even if you're not feeling that way on the inside. This preserves an essence of professionalism in any situation. For instance, when you walk into a meeting room, you communicate to others immediately whether or not you have presence. Walking in slowly and assuredly, greeting others with eye contact, smiling and saying hello communicates confidence immediately.

YOUR INVISIBLE TOOLBOX

Your professional presence is established one interaction at a time. Slowing down is a tool you can plug and play today.

Slow down

37

TWO SECONDS TO SUCCESS OR FAILURE

Research from Harvard University reveals that you will form an opinion of a new person or experience in about two seconds. In fact, people will size you up and make inferences about your competence in those two seconds based on visual qualities such as your height, weight, age, skin color, gender.

Additional research reveals that:

· Tall people are perceived to be more credible than short people.

· Men are perceived to be more capable in crisis (particularly a physical crisis) than women.

· Older people are perceived to be resistant to change or adverse to technology.

· Younger people are perceived to be entitled and self-centered.

Malcolm Gladwell, in his book *Blink*, cites the following staggering statistics as evidence of the bias our society has for one visual quality—height. Only 14.5 percent of American men are over six feet tall, yet more than 58 percent of Fortune 500 CEOs are that height. Gladwell's research also revealed that fewer than 4 percent of adult men are six foot two or taller while nearly a third of the CEOs in his study were six foot two or taller.

It should be noted that there have been no studies that reveal a correlation between height and qualities important for CEOs to possess, such as intelligence, competence, integrity, or credibility.

People tend to think that attractive people are smarter, friendlier, more honest and reliable than less attractive people. They associate one positive thing (attractiveness) with many other good things (intelligence).

Interviewers are often impressed with a great communicator and attach a number of other skills to the job candidate that he or she may not possess, such as integrity and sales ability. When interviewers are so impressed with a candidate that they overlook negative qualities—often rationalizing that they are trainable—this is called the Halo Effect.

The opposite is the Horns Effect. Someone who doesn't make a good first impression is often thought more poorly of in areas where he or she does have strengths. For example, a poor visual impression can cause others to attribute negative qualities, such as lack of intelligence or motivation to the interviewee, though neither may be true.

Early impressions form lasting impressions.

There is good news. Your grooming and attire also make a powerful first impression and are completely within your control.

Research continues to show that all people, regardless of gender, are judged by their appearance. This is a fact not likely to change in a single generation, even by a cohort as large as the millennials. We can bemoan this reality or we can choose to leverage what the research tells us about how people form perceptions. We've all seen talented professionals lose out on a promotion to a seemingly less qualified individual who exudes executive presence—from entry level to an executive position. The comfort of wearing whatever you want is small reward if you've been overlooked for your dream job.

When you look like an expert at what you do, you will visually command and convey respect.
BECKY RUPIPER-GREENE

We perceive ourselves in our best light. We judge ourselves by our good intentions. Others can't see our good intentions. They first see the visual image we broadcast to the world, and that plays a huge role in how they judge us.

When you look unsure and unkempt, people will react to you with reluctance. When you look polished and professional, you will encounter respect. Before long, you'll not only be enjoying the results, you'll be embracing the positive perceptions internally as well.

YOUR INVISIBLE TOOLBOX

Are you making the most of your two seconds? Is your visual presence communicating positively for you?

Maximize your visual impression

—————————————— 38 ——————————————

DITCH THE DRESS CODE

*That blouse may get you a second glance on the corporate elevator
but may cost you a second chance on the corporate ladder.*
BECKY RUPIPER-GREENE

For many millennials, one of the appealing characteristics about a workplace is a casual dress code. Millennials are not alone in this interest. It seems a push for more casual attire has also come from gen Xers and boomers. The interesting dilemma dress code presents is that your visual image is over half of what makes up how people perceive you. If your goal is to be comfortable, the casual dress code works. If your goal is to be taken seriously and to look capable and confident, it may not.

Tero's image expert, Becky Rupiper-Greene, contends there are two things that should drive the decision on how we attire ourselves. Neither one is the dress code. She states, "Visit the ER before you visit your business meeting." ER is an acronym. The "E" stands for "look like an *Expert* in what you do." The "R" stands for "that can *Relate* to what they do." Expertise and relatability. Forget the dress code. Ask yourself if you look like an expert and if others can relate to you.

Some considerations are nonnegotiable if you want to be taken seriously, in particular the impact your appearance has on the way you're perceived by others. Whether you're meeting with a customer, engaging a prospective client, seeking to impress senior leaders, or interacting with a colleague, strategic impression management on your part has the potential to shape relationships in a positive manner.

Consider just a few seemingly small details that make a significant difference in the impression others form of you:

　　• Shoes are one of the first things people notice, so always put your best foot forward. Are they appropriate for the occasion? Do they need to be polished, resoled, or laces replaced? Are they a current or classic style? Dated or scuffed shoes imply that your products, services, or knowledge may also be lacking or dated as well.

• Your hands are on display constantly, whether shaking someone else's, pointing to information on a report, or eating with colleagues in a restaurant. Keeping your hands clean and nails well-trimmed is essential. Neglected hands suggest potential neglect elsewhere.

• Unflattering or dated eyewear can have a negative influence on your visual message. Avoid wearing tinted glasses indoors as they can make you look tired in addition to inhibiting good eye contact.

You are your number one asset and thus worth investing in. When you invest in yourself, others are willing to invest in you. Recent research done by economists who studied the correlation between time spent grooming and wages revealed that every extra ten minutes of daily grooming increases weekly wages for men by 6 percent. Women need to increase grooming time slightly more to achieve similar returns.

When you take care of your impression management, you'll see the result as an increase in confidence, self-esteem, and effectiveness. Personal effectiveness inevitably leads to organizational effectiveness and success—a winning result for all.

YOUR INVISIBLE TOOLBOX

Ask yourself, do I look promotable? Do my shoes, nails, eyewear, attire, and image communicate my professionalism?

Dress like a relatable expert

39

WHAT'S UP WITH YOUR VOICE?

Can your voice affect if you get hired or promoted?

A study by Florida Atlantic University found that women who had vocal fry were perceived as less competent, less educated, less trustworthy, and less hirable. Vocal fry, a particular pattern of speech made famous by Kim Kardashian, Brittany Spears, and Katy Perry, among others, is a pervasive vocal trend among millennials.

On the Osborne Head and Neck Institute website, Dr. Reena Gupta explains, "The lowest of the vocal registers is fry. It occurs when the vocal cartilages are squeezed tightly. The cords themselves remain loose and floppy, rattling against each other when air passes through, resulting in a creaky voice."

In layman's terms it sounds as if the voice lowers at the end of a word, sentence, or thought. Vocal fry is characteristic in the United Kingdom in males and communicates a hyper masculinity. For millennial women, it may be communicating just the opposite depending on who's listening.

The issue with this mode of speaking is that it becomes a habit that is difficult to change. You can dress appropriately for an interview, but it's not as easy switching up your vocal pattern if it's an ingrained habit.

A University of Louisiana study found that when tested to say normal words, 86 percent of women indicated vocal fry. Diane DiResta, a communication expert, has stated that "adolescent girls are subconsciously adopting this speech pattern, and it's limiting their employment opportunities."

How can it limit opportunity? It gets in the way of the message being heard and is a pattern not every generation is familiar with hearing.

Dr. Penny Eckert, professor of linguistics at Stanford University, was quoted as saying, "I was shocked the first time I heard this style on NPR. I thought, 'Oh my God, how can this person be talking like this on the radio?' Then I played it for my students and said, 'How does she sound?' and they said, 'Good, authoritative.' That was when I knew I had a problem...that I was not a part of the generation that understood what that style means...There's been a change, and those of us who are bothered by some of these features are probably just getting old."

Another speech pattern that also challenges positive perceptions people may form of us is "upspeak." Upspeak speakers don't descend with their voices but instead go upward at the end of sentences and thoughts, essentially turning everything into a question. This style can unintentionally convey tentativeness or a lack of confidence.

> *The human voice is the most beautiful instrument of all,*
> *but it is the most difficult to play.*
> RICHARD STRAUSS

According to feminist Naomi Wolf, "Vocal fry has joined more traditional young-women voice mannerisms such as run-ons, breathiness, and the dreaded question marks in sentences (upspeak) to undermine these women's authority in newly distinctive ways."

Will you benefit from people thinking, "What's up with your voice?" Or is there greater return leveraging this powerful instrument to transcend assumptions, opinions, and generations so that it works as a tool for getting you hired?

YOUR INVISIBLE TOOLBOX

It may be useful to record your voice. Then ask yourself, "What are my vocal quality patterns? What do they communicate about me?"

Audit your voice

40

FINDING YOUR VOICE

Florence and the Machine. Adele. Michael Jackson. Whitney Houston. Patsy Cline. Orson Welles. Luciano Pavarotti. Katharine Hepburn. Lauren Bacall. James Earl Jones. Marilyn Monroe. Ted Williams. What do these people have in common?

Most of us could not sit on the side of a road with a sign saying "I have a God-given gift of a great voice, wait until you hear it" and ever be offered a job, a home, and tens of thousands of dollars. But that was Ted Williams' experience. For the homeless man with the golden voice, life changed in an instant. His voice changed his life.

We underestimate the power that the voice has in serving a colleague or customer. The same regions of the brain that process intonations in our voice also play a large role in figuring out and creating emotions. Because of this, your voice tone has a huge impact on another person's emotional state.

Chances are you've experienced unpleasant outcomes when speaking in front of others while nervous. Is that such a big deal?

It is a big deal and an even bigger one if you're communicating via the phone. In phone conversations, people can't see you. Several research studies have shown that as much as 87 percent of the opinions people have about you are based on vocal quality and only 13 percent on the words spoken.

Jeannie Campbell, a Tero International vocal coach, states, "The voice is a complex mechanism capable of producing over three hundred different pitches. There are more nerves in the muscles of the larynx than any other muscles in your body except your eyes. Given that you use approximately three-quarters of your body to utter a word, is it any wonder that your voice can be adversely affected by excitement and stress?"

In basic terms, the voice is produced using breath, vocal folds, and head resonance—or the modifying of the sound waves as they bounce off hard and soft tissue in the throat, mouth, and nose.

These three areas specifically can be affected by stress or nervousness, causing the voice to shake or to become thin and strained. Even if a person is not particularly nervous, he or she may possess undesirable vocal qualities that cause him or her to be perceived negatively.

One of the most important elements of vocal quality is tone.

From the moment we are born, and before we learn language as a communication tool, we make connections. These connections are based largely on what we hear. A mother's soothing voice leads to an emotion of comfort. Loud or unexpected noises can lead to emotions of fear.

How is it different for adults who have the full use of verbal language? Evidently not much. We look for alignment in communication, but when the message delivered is not congruent with the vocal delivery, we trust the delivery as the true message.

A psychologist at Harvard compared the office manner of surgeons who had been sued multiple times with those who had never been sued. Doctors with "a more dominant tone of voice," were more likely to have been sued by patients. Doctors whose voices contained more warmth were less likely to have been sued.

When a person says "bad doggie" to a puppy in a kind and loving voice, the puppy hears "good doggie." Tone sends a message. Your pets can tell a lot from the volume, tone, and vocal inflection you use when you talk to them.

YOUR INVISIBLE TOOLBOX

Tone of voice is more important than the words said. Infants are experts in interpreting communication. It's safe to say your colleagues, employees, customers, and leaders do the same thing.

Monitor your vocal tone

41

YOU WON!

Millennials, it is thought, want to be recognized more often than other generations. They also feel recognition is best if it's personalized. In fact, they would prefer to be able to choose the awards they get, keeping them in line with their personal goals and lives.

Recognition comes in many forms in the workplace. Traditionally, at the highest levels, it is in the form of an award. Be it the Presidential Medal of Freedom, an Academy Award, Top Sales Person or Company Humanitarian, awards are given in a variety of contexts and for a variety of reasons.

There is more hunger for love and appreciation in this world than for bread.
MOTHER TERESA

For recipients, awards serve not only as external motivators, but they also gratify psychological needs such as recognition, social status, and self-fulfillment. Presenters use these public honors to motivate employees, create social linkages, and develop positive interactions with the award honorees and the community in general.

Accepting an award showcases talent and achievement. Unfortunately, many people ruin their reputation by not accepting an award well. Instead, they let the occasion of receiving be an excuse to get on stage and talk.

What if you are the recipient of an achievement award? What do you need to know to accept the award with as much savviness as you had to earn it?

The savvy winners at awards ceremonies are concise and appreciative in their remarks. They typically place their thanks into three brief categories: the process that enabled the award, the people they worked with, or an influential leader who paved the way.

Following the technique of three guarantees there's no risk of a spontaneous bad joke or reference or the risk of going on too long—which everyone will notice. This is not the time to go over a long list of names to thank. An award is for the recipient, not for relatives and friends.

Preparing ahead of time for the awards you have coming in your future is wise.

YOUR INVISIBLE TOOLBOX

Accepting an award creates a designated public showcase for you to define your professionalism, as well as get the credit you deserve.

Prepare for recognition

42

WHO WANTS TO SIT WHEN WE CAN CLIMB?

You can sit on the step of entitlement or get on the ladder of success.
BECKY RUPIPER-GREENE

The new hires had no idea what was really going on. Gathered in the auditorium for their first onboarding experience, they were eagerly chatting and getting to know one another. As the speakers began, they settled into the first topic of onboarding.

In the back of the room were their leaders, the individuals who would pave the way for their success. These were the people they would learn under, grow under, and ultimately potentially exceed.

Once the onboarding speeches on the stage commenced, the leaders in the back began to look at each new hire. How? A virtual field trip. Typing in the names of the candidates on their computers, they were able to view what came up alongside each name. Wandering out to Facebook. Taking a look at their tweets and LinkedIn presence.

Occasionally a leader would turn to another and point at something. There were smiles as they looked at the online presence of their new charges but also some looks of concern.

Ninety-five percent of this new hire group was fresh out of college. Although they had obviously made sure they were dressed appropriately for work the first day and conducted themselves well as they briefly met the leadership group, many forgot to take care of one thing. They hadn't considered someone would be looking to see if their online presence reflected the qualities and values they were hired for and the organization stood for.

We could argue that one's social media presence, especially when it comes to Facebook or Twitter or Instagram, belongs to each of us personally and we can post what we want. We could argue that we don't have a responsibility to be professional in the aspects of our lives not connected to work.

Yet if what people see of us online doesn't align with the experience they have with us in person, could there be a disconnect and could the disconnect affect trust?

Cleaning up our online presence is as necessary to success as monitoring our daily appearance and quality of our work. It all adds up to create the impression we make. Who wants to sit when we can climb?

Online presence is something worth monitoring. Imagine someone checking out your online accounts. Would the impression they get be favorable?

YOUR INVISIBLE TOOLBOX

Checking privacy settings, removing outdated or questionable photos, and treating your online presence as a vehicle for someone to get to know the professional you matters.

Audit your online presence

—————————— 43 ——————————

THE MESSAGE AND THE MESSENGER

*In the past, it was always about brands talking at people
and sending out simple, repetitive messaging. But because of the way
millennials constantly interact with tech and social networking, they are
literally inundated with messaging. Some say they are immune to it.
It's like they all have mental spam-blockers to help them filter
(and ignore) the avalanche. But what is able to get through to them is
firsthand experience. They want to feel your brand—not hear it.
They want to interact with it, play with it, pass it on and discuss it
with their friends. They want to understand what it stands for and how
it can make their lives better. And it's your job to help them do it.*
SANDY THOMPSON

Individuals and organizations invest heavily in the development of messages they want delivered. Whether it's a marketing department seeking the perfect way to present a new product to consumers or a leader seeking to inspire a group with a powerful message, words are important. However, people rarely trust the message if they don't trust the messenger.

How can a messenger build trust with listeners? The task is challenging and is made even more so when the interaction is new, brief, or occurs at a time of tension in a relationship.

Have you ever seen excellent ideas get rejected because of poor communication of those ideas? Or ideas of less merit being accepted because they were delivered by a great communicator? Are ideas accepted based on logic and facts alone?

In a world where individuals are overloaded with information, it's no longer enough to simply communicate information. Success ultimately depends on the speaker's ability to communicate confidently and persuasively in a variety of settings.

A great message in the hands of a poor messenger does not produce desired results. In his book *Rhetoric*, Aristotle described the three things required to persuade another person to act. One must appeal to *logos* (Greek word meaning "logic"), to *pathos* (Greek word meaning "emotions"), and to *ethos* (Greek word meaning "disposition" or "character"). In other words, for the message delivery to be successful, the information must make sense, evoke desirable emotions, and be delivered by someone trusted. Kouzes and Posner, authors of *The Leadership Challenge*, point out that you won't believe the message if you don't trust the messenger.

To persuade is the goal of every message we send. Whether we're selling an idea, a concept, a product, a service, or our own credibility, we want our listener to buy. We want people to trust us and the information we're communicating.

The most important element of persuasion is trust. If I like you, trust you, and have confidence in you, I will likely do what you suggest or believe what you say—even if it doesn't make logical sense.

The natural tendency of human beings is to justify on facts but buy on feelings. People tend to do business with people they like, trust, and have confidence in.

Even though millennials are known to make more carefully and better informed buying decisions than generations of the past, there are still people who can get them to buy things they shouldn't buy or do things they shouldn't do. They know how to leverage the skills to appear to be the kind of person people can trust. In the long term, their deception is nearly always revealed. In the short term, the damage caused can be shattering to those who believe the messenger.

Ensuring congruence between your credible message and your desire to be perceived as a credible messenger is critical.

YOUR INVISIBLE TOOLBOX

All research indicates that the impression you make as a professional is far more important than the words you actually say. So why do you spend so much time working on the content of your message and so little attention to your delivery style and environment? Of course the content must be sound, well thought through, and tailored to the people you're speaking to. But poor communication can destroy an otherwise technically flawless message. The opposite holds true as well; superior delivery can sometimes save a weak message. Unfair—and true.

Focus on message delivery

Part III

TOOLS FOR WORKING GLOBALLY

Whether you're in Des Moines or Dubai, twenty-first century business requires you to competently interact and communicate with clients and colleagues of different cultures. On a plane, at a meeting, on the phone, or by the water cooler, you simply cannot afford to make a misunderstood gesture, drop an ill-placed phrase, or use uninformed judgment. What you don't know can, and indeed will, hurt you. What you think you know is usually filtered by what you have experienced.

Understanding, appreciating, and maximizing the benefits of cultural differences due to geography or generation are critical to achievement in the domestic or global marketplace. The professional in today's workplace faces a multitude of high-level challenges and questions daily due to culture and diversity.

In this part of the book, we examine the tools for working cross-culturally.

We don't see things as they are; we see them as we are.
ANAIS NIN

44

HUNGRY FOR A BIG MAC

Navigating culture in the workplace isn't easy. Even though the millennial generation is cited as being more inclusive due to growing up in more diverse environments than generations past, is the feeling of being inclusive and the actual demonstration of it always aligned?

Years ago many businesses decided to roll out their successful US models to countries abroad. McDonald's was one of them. Who wouldn't like a Big Mac and a shake? McDonald's was at the top of their game domestically. Certainly what was beloved in the United States would be beloved around the world.

Wrong. McDonald's found out very quickly that people in India didn't care for beef sandwiches and that in France they preferred to have wine rather than a shake.

We're living in a whole new social and economic order with a whole new set of problems and challenges. Old assumptions and old programs don't work in this new society, and the more we try to stretch them to make them fit, the more we will be seen as running away from what is reality.
ANN RICHARDS

McDonald's got the message, albeit after the fact. They realized that when it comes to culture, one size doesn't fit all, even if it's supersized.

McDonald's took a critical look at their business model. They did the two things each of us is required to do when it comes to cultural differences. First, they reexamined their values. What is valued in the United States may be in conflict with a value in a culturally different location. Second, they challenged their assumptions. McDonald's rolled out the US model assuming it would be what people desired. What other assumptions were they in need of challenging?

Today we find chicken burgers made of thigh meat in China, as well as a Happy New Year Meal that includes the Chinese horoscope. In Japan, shrimp nuggets and hot dogs are served for a breakfast meal. That's what the Japanese consumer appreciates. McCurry Pan, a curried vegetable medley, can be found in every McDonald's in India, all of which are predominately vegetarian restaurants.

Working to understand what is valued culturally informs. It also affects success. With 67.7 percent of McDonald's business happening outside the United States, aligning the intent to be inclusive with actually providing for different palates and expectations made sense, as it does for all of us when dealing with difference.

Don't make assumptions about your culturally different colleagues. Instead, ask questions and find out what they value. Reexamining your own values doesn't mean changing them, it just means evaluating them in light of someone else's and reflecting on other ways of looking at the world. In doing so you'll open yourself to lining up who you think others are with what you foster in reality.

YOUR INVISIBLE TOOLBOX

What assumptions do you have about a particular culture or people? Can you challenge yourself to challenge those assumptions and find out if they are founded?

Challenge your assumptions

45

CAN I EAT FRENCH FRIES WITH MY FINGERS?

According to Restaurant Marketing Labs, millennials like to dine out. Look at what they found:

- 2.45 trillion: The spending power of millennials.
- $174: Amount millennials spend on eating out per month on average. Non-millennials spend $153 per month.
- 55: The percentage of millennials who prefer communal tables at restaurants.
- 87: The percentage of millennials who will "splurge on a nice meal, even when money is tight."
- 68: The percentage of millennials who will ask friends before picking a restaurant.
- 40: The percentage of millennials who will order different things every time they visit the same restaurant. Millennials like variety.
- 60: The percentage of millennials who follow brands (including restaurants chains) they like on social media to hear about new deals or coupons.
- 56: The percentage of millennials in America who would share their location (on apps like Foursquare) to receive a deal at a restaurant.

"Millennials dine out a lot," affirms Sara Monnette, director of consumer research at foodservice research firm Technomic. "In terms of spending, they're not the biggest spenders at restaurants because they don't have as much disposable income, but they are dining out frequently. And based on where they are in their lives—a lot are moving back home, living with parents, living in multigenerational households—they tend to use restaurants as a place to gather with their friends."

She goes on to state, in an article by Full Service Menu magazine, "Forty-one percent of millennials purchase food away from home at least twice a week, compared to 38 percent of Gen Xers and 37 percent of baby boomers."

With all that dining out, the restaurant experience is a natural until the opportunity comes to conduct business over a meal. Dining is kinesthetic; the chance our clients remember us and what we had to promote is magnified when they remember it in the context of a meal. The memories aren't always positive when we put cultural difference in the mix.

> *Food is a central activity of mankind and one of the*
> *single most significant trademarks of a culture.*
> MARK KURLANSKY

Expectations around dining exist, and most people feel their mode of interacting with food, drink, and guests at the table is right. We eat several times a day, so certainly we know how to dine. Eating is ingesting. Dining is an experience. The food is the vehicle for something more. Culture skews them both and requires us to pay attention.

- Do I leave a bad impression if I eat my French fries with my fingers?
- If the salad is served last, can I ask for mine before my meal?
- Do I really have to eat that fish with the eyes looking up at me?

The dining landscape when we are with internationals or on business internationally can feel really foreign. Hidden expectations and rules can ruin the impression we leave without us even realizing it. Failure to recognize the cues can hurt us. There are places in Europe where you need to use your knife and fork with fries. Salad may be last at a formal banquet because that's French service, and we cannot rearrange the order! When in Asia, we compliment our host by eating the fish, as they planned this special treat just for us.

Most of us have heard the phrase "Hurry up and eat!" That doesn't work when dining cross-culturally. Paying attention to those around you, how they engage with their meal and utensils, can be the only translation you have for what's happening at the table. You think you know dining because you dine a lot. Translating when working with internationals is taking your cues from those around you.

YOUR INVISIBLE TOOLBOX

When you begin a meal with internationals, don't concentrate on feeding yourself. Pay attention to how others are engaging with their food and take cues.

Follow your host

46

TRICKING HUMAN NATURE

It is human nature to form perceptions quickly based on immediate value judgments. No one is the victim of this more than the millennial generation. You can't google a term without it being associated with millennials in some form. Whether you agree with the perception or not, there it is. The same thing happens when you work with people culturally different than yourself.

The issue with doing this is that people may evaluate incorrectly and react based on the judgment rather than reality. It's probably happened to you as a millennial, and it's something you have most likely done to someone else. It definitely happens when working cross-culturally.

Man is too quick at forming conclusions.
EDWARD E. BARNARD

How can you avoid making these immediate value judgments? By using description, interpretation, and evaluation as a perception-checking strategy.

- Description: When confronted with something new, you should first observe it without evaluating. Chances are that you'll then be able to describe it.
- Interpretation: Describing gives you the ability to consider all the possibilities that may explain what you're seeing or experiencing rather than judging it. This is the interpretation phase.
- Evaluation: After interpreting something, you can evaluate it more clearly and correctly.

The tendency to evaluate behavior from another person, generation, or culture as good or bad is to make a judgment based on your own cultural or personal bias. Evaluation has been called the third stage of how we all attribute meaning. The first two, description and interpretation, lead naturally to it.

Different attitudes about food or drink, for instance, can cause misunderstanding as you evaluate them.

If your cultural or personal programming encompasses the belief that people should eat neatly and quietly, you may find eating habits that are noisy and communal difficult. You might evaluate someone eating noisily as rude or uncivilized.

This would clearly be judging rather than describing. It would be skipping the interpretation phase in which thinking of possible reasons the behavior is occurring (possible cultural difference?) might clue you in to why it's happening and keep you from jumping to assessing from your own programming and lens.

The goal in responding to difference is to describe, interpret, and evaluate. Yet it is our inclination to go right into evaluating. How can we decrease the tendency to evaluate? Gaining insight into our own values and what makes us tick.

YOUR INVISIBLE TOOLBOX

Describe, interpret, evaluate is the perception-checking strategy that ensures you will not form judgments about behavior but rather try to interpret behavior.

Describe, interpret, evaluate

47

I NEVER KNEW YOU FELT THAT WAY

Cross-cultural misunderstandings are more prevalent than you think. If you say or do something that offends someone, and it has a cultural implication, chances are it won't be discussed. Consider these three cases, all true, with the names changed to protect the innocent but with permission given to share.

Case One

Louis was a French information technology manager hired by a small US West Coast firm. In France, hierarchy is demonstrated through expertise. So being the IT head of this firm was a true source of pride. One day, Louis was walking down the hall, where the president of the company, the controller, and a few others were standing around talking. As Louis approached, the president summoned him into the group and excitedly introduced an idea for IT he had read about over the weekend. The president felt this new technology would benefit the business and wanted to look into it. Louis was stunned, for in France, this type of informal discussion wouldn't be happening, because, by the way, he was the expert in IT. Why was the president discussing this? Louis should have been the one to promote a new idea.

Case Two

Lanying was originally from China but now worked on a US manufacturing team. In China, Lanying had learned from an early age to always converse in a way that didn't formally disagree with anyone. You never said anything that would cause someone to do what in China is called "losing face." Lanying was the brains of her team. Often the team held brainstorming discussions to determine if they should invest in a particular product or process. When the consensus was arrived at, Lanying's boss would look to her and ask if she agreed. He knew her opinion and decision were the ones to listen to. Put on the spot, if Lanying didn't agree, she would say, "We could try." To her that meant "no," but to her US boss it sounded like validation for the idea and was a green light.

Case Three

Peter was assigned to his company's office in Germany. A competent manager in the United States, he was expected to be a skilled expatriate manager who would bridge the expectations and understandings of the German counterparts with the home office. Peter took his assignment seriously and desired to create "one company" regardless of geographical distance. Upon arrival to the German offices, Peter noticed that all of the individual office doors stayed closed throughout the day. In the United States the home office had just been renovated to reflect a shared, inclusive modern workplace. Communal work areas were designed to enhance collaboration. Peter decided one of the first things to do was to request that everyone open their office doors because that was how things were done in the United States.

> *If we are going to live with our deepest differences then we*
> *must learn about one another.*
> DEBORAH J. LEVINE

In each of these cases, the misunderstanding was not communicated. It was just felt.

- Louis didn't tell the president how upset he was. In fact, why it upset him wasn't even completely clear to him; he just knew the situation prompted some terrible feelings, and he questioned if his expertise was valued.
- In the case of Lanying, telling her boss she was uncomfortable saying no due to the fact that she was a high-context communicator wasn't an option. In her native language, Mandarin, there is no single character or word that means no, and by saying "we could try" she was really saying "no."

• For Peter, no one complained to him when they had to adjust their preference of having office doors closed even though that was the norm in the German office. They did, however, register the idea that it was his way or the highway, and they surmised he would not be respectful of what mattered to them. Thus the feeling he created and knew nothing about affected his leadership and success as an expat.

Silence is said to be golden. The unfortunate aspect of silence prompted by cross-cultural misunderstanding is that it really isn't silent. The volume of discontent and the feelings of shame and mistrust are loud and clear on the inside of individuals. Because cultural norms and ways run so deep within us, we often cannot find the words to express the problem in the issue. Wouldn't it be great if through cultural understanding we could avoid the issues altogether?

YOUR INVISIBLE TOOLBOX

Be on the lookout for potential cross-cultural misunderstandings. Building relationships with those culturally different from you can yield dividends in learning to understand cultural nuances.

Learn about culture

48

JUMPING INTO THE POOL

Millennials are being asked to join a particularly challenging succession pool in order to take the reins of retiring global leaders. A shortage of global executives is the number one business challenge while global assignments expand. Millennials are succeeding individuals who have developed their global skillset over time, yet they are expected to hit the ground running without the benefit of a skillset from experience to draw on.

Will you end up like Joe?

Joe felt pretty optimistic at the conclusion of his sales presentation to a Japanese client. The client paused and thoughtfully said, "Ah, yes." Joe assumed the client was ready to buy.

What Joe did not know was that in his client's culture, "no" or contrary thoughts are not always expressed directly, in so many words, or to a person's face. Nonverbal cues (such as the long pause) can be as valid and communicative as words spoken aloud to cultures that rely on implicit messages rather than explicit explanations.

It has been said that when Americans want to say one hundred things, they verbalize 150 things, for they are explicit in their use of language in communication. When the Japanese verbalize seventy things, they are trying to get the other person to understand one hundred, for they are using implicit understandings and at times nonverbal cues to get their point across.

What are the differences in verbal communication that are rooted in culture? How do they influence our success in doing business internationally?

Edward T. Hall, a cultural anthropologist, found that cultures can be separated into two groups with regard to communication. High-context cultures (such as East Asian, Latin American, Southern Mediterranean, and Arab countries) are commonly homogeneous and share a history of common values and assumptions passed on by strong family structure and educational systems.

When people of high-context cultures communicate, it is not necessary for them to say everything explicitly; rather, a kind of shorthand can be used (similar to how we communicate within our families). Nonverbal cues often communicate what is not said, and silence can have great meaning.

In low-context cultures (such as American, Canadian, and Western European countries), communicators tend to verbalize background information, prefer clear descriptions and unambiguous communication, and are highly specific. Low-context communicators do not often rely on or trust shared understandings in business communications.

How does this play out when high- and low-context business persons go about communicating?

- High-context communicators might assume a greater level of shared understanding than actually exists, thus communicating in a fashion that can appear ambiguous to low-context folks. Because of their approach to communication, people of high-context cultures can sometimes be unjustly regarded as sneaky or nondisclosing. And, like Joe's Japanese client, high-context communicators might infuse important nonverbal messages and seemingly misleading comments that have implicit meaning.

- On the other hand, low-context communicators can appear excessively talkative and redundant. When talking to a high-context person, they appear to be saying things they would not need to if there were a shared understanding. Too often we look to our cultural counterparts to answer us back with the same enthusiasm for speech and background information we feel compelled to provide.

How can we bridge this communication gap?

The gap is more about the language of behavior than language use itself. It can be bridged by focusing on the key necessary to unlocking business in any form and at any level—relationships.

Preservation of one's own culture does not require contempt
or disrespect for other cultures.
CESAR CHAVEZ

High-context cultures value the relationship, and knowing the history and character of who they are dealing with can be as important as the facts of the deal itself. A solid relationship supports a high-context culture's natural implicit communication preference, thus it is to our advantage to devote time and attention to relationship building early in the process.

Low-context communicators must recognize that they may be perceived as moving too fast and overly talkative. This can inform them to slow down, approach the communication through developing understandings rather than just by giving explanations, and let relationships percolate before trying to seal (or even propose) the deal.

YOUR INVISIBLE TOOLBOX

What context do you use to form your messages? Low context or high context? What experiences can you give yourself to begin to understand the alternate context? When establishing business in high-context regions (such as Asia), relationship building can be the most critical initial component. Contextual difference in communication styles is just one of the reasons why.

Consider contextual difference

49

THE FAST TRACK

It is said millennials want global assignments, to move ahead into leadership rapidly, and are willing to take short-term assignments to make this happen. The challenge in a rapid track to global leadership is in its requirements. The skills and management expertise needed when working in your own culture are one thing. When working cross-culturally, your world view is going to play a part in your success, and if you've never considered this fact, you may be in for a surprise.

Most likely someone you are working or interacting with holds a personal world view different than your own.

Can that affect behavior, expectations, and your leadership? Absolutely! Positively or negatively depending on how you leverage the differences.

In her book *International Dimensions of Organizational Behavior*, Nancy Adler explores the complexities differing cultural world views can have on leaders in the workplace.

Adler suggests reflecting on the following to become aware of the part culture plays in global leadership.

- What are the cultural beliefs and attitudes you have about life and work? (Think back to messages received as a child).
- How does cultural upbringing hinder or help your ability to work with others different than yourself under your organizational structure?
- How are your beliefs similar or different from your organization's culture?

A people without the knowledge of their past history, origin, and culture are like a tree without roots.
MARCUS GARVEY

Identify value and cultural differences of those working around you. Commonly the differences lie in the following areas:

- How one perceives the use of time: One thing at a time business focus or many things occurring and relationships taking precedence
- Communication: Direct to the point or more embedded in a lot of context and consideration of the "face" and feelings of the receiver
- Perceptions of power and hierarchy: Addressing and responding to people with regard to position or more equalitarian and less concerned with power
- Predominant relationship or task completion emphasis
- Individualistic (own self) or collectivistic (group orientation)

Once you've identified value and cultural differences in those working around you, ask yourself, what did I learn?

The first step toward global competency and an inclusive worldview is knowing yourself and what you were taught to hold as valuable personal work behaviors and outcomes.

Step two is being able to see that differences *do* exist. This can best be facilitated by asking those around you what they value and how it is demonstrated through their work.

There's no need to be threatened by differing values and views. You do, however, have a responsibility to figure out what value differences exist in your workplace.

The twenty-first-century leader and valued employee is one who has the ability to manage difference and ambiguity through understanding value differences and differing world views. If you desire rapid opportunity, the time to do this work is now.

YOUR INVISIBLE TOOLBOX

Until you examine your own world view, you will find it challenging to be inclusive of those you lead. Ask yourself, what do you value in the workplace based on your cultural upbringing?

Understand your worldview

50

WHERE IN THE WORLD ARE WE?

When technology and distance comprise our team environment, chances are we are only meeting virtually. Virtual teams can differ in their experiences from a team that meets face-to-face. Generational differences can also be more difficult if they're present in the mix, as millennials don't always expect or need the same things from the team environment as others do.

Team experience in a virtual environment makes it difficult to create something that can also be easily lost.

Trust.

Although trust is a foundation for any relationship, it plays a particularly important role in virtual team dynamics.

Virtual teams can be defined as either function teams, which address business operations and are ongoing, or project teams, which are formed to work on a specific project over time and have a clear objective. There are also task force teams, which meet to accomplish a short-term goal like a recommendation for a particular issue.

Knowing purpose and recognizing scope is the first step to forming a team that understands its accountability. This allows a team to set parameters and begin to communicate in the mode(s) most useful to achieve the goals yet support the individuals. Communication that is clear and team members who know their role can set the wheels of swift trust in motion.

What cultural groups are represented on your team? What are the values of each? Where do the team members line up as to communication style, orientation to task, view of power, individualism or group perspective, and time orientation? Knowing the cultural variances will help you set inclusive guidelines.

With respect to culture comes an attention to generational diversity as well. Maybe it isn't national culture you must deal with but generational. Are some members of your team more tech savvy? Do others have more institutional knowledge that will be critical? Dialoguing best practice—leveraging all the differences to create processes that instill trust—is paramount to success.

Mindsets across generations and cultures vary. A meeting of the minds is essential if you are to escape potential misunderstanding. Figuring out what you as a team member need to value to ensure you reach your maximum potential is key. What aspects of the various mindsets will be most conducive to reaching your goal?

Terence Brake, author of *Where in the World Is My Team?*, identified nine personal qualities that prepare the soil for trust among team members in a virtual environment.

1. Respect
2. Openness
3. Transparency
4. Integrity
5. Empathy
6. Caring
7. Confidence
8. Congeniality
9. Reciprocity

Unfortunately, these words mean different things to those with cultural and generational differences. Find out by asking the simple question "What do these mean to you?" before assuming that the same definition and expectation will streamline potential pitfalls.

Tolerance, intercultural dialogue, and respect for diversity are more essential than ever in a world where peoples are becoming more and more closely interconnected.
KOFI ANNAN

Risk and complexity can unseat many a noble idea or action. If your goal involves either, you will need to overcommunicate in order to maintain trust. What does that mean? Every step of the process will need to be communicated well, opened for discussion, clarified, and checked for understanding with all team members.

Virtual teams require more trust than face-to-face teams, as the ability to misunderstand others is greater when remote. If problems crop up, you can always circle back to discussions around how best to communicate in order to give and get trust. Establishing trust is not a once and done. In the mix of generation, culture, and task, the opportunity to hone your teaming skills is second to the chance to elevate your ability to bring diverse minds and roles together.

YOUR INVISIBLE TOOLBOX

Being skilled in the technical aspects of what the task requires can foster the component that will make or break success: team dynamics.

Develop swift trust

51

GETTING THE MIX TO WORK

Studies have shown millennials view diversity as the blending of different backgrounds, experiences, and perspectives within a team, which is known as cognitive diversity. Where it's comforting to think that everyone acts "cognitively" when in situations and interactions with diverse team members, each slice of what makes a team diverse is in fact its own operative and can have its own effect. Take the case of Korean Air.

Unfortunately, many businesses have to restructure under the eyes of a watching public. Probably none more vividly than Korean Air. In the 1990s Korean Air had a series of traumatic events. By far the worst of twelve serious accidents that occurred in this time frame was the loss of a Boeing 747, which crash landed in Guam in 1997, killing 227 people.

Although there were some external conditions that could have contributed to the crash, none of them were enough to merit a catastrophe of this size. During investigation it was found that in flight, the major errors occurred in the cockpit and were directly caused by the relationship the pilots had to each other and to cultural expectations.

One known generalization concerning Korean culture is that life is characterized by hierarchy, respect for elders, and rank. So much so that the crew might defer to the highest-ranking pilot. In this case, the pilot was reported to be confused as to communications, did not follow safety protocol, and was reportedly sleepy. What should have been a team approach of the crew with respect to aviation protocol, which may have compensated for this problem, became an ill-fated mistake due to people acting and reacting based on cultural values.

Even a technically skilled pilot with rigid protocols can succumb to the effects of national culture on the job, to the point where he or she does not operate with a totally unbiased capacity. The product, in this case a safe trip for the passengers, is jeopardized. It's said that for an employee, national culture, its expectations, and values, will trump organizational culture.

"We realized we needed to concentrate more on 'how' we fly and less on 'where' we are flying to." This is a quote from a top official for the owners of Korean Airlines after the fact. Unfortunately, this quote is a metaphor for how we often operate in business: looking forward to where we're going and forgetting that how we proceed is going to eventually win out in determining our success. Knowledge of cultural difference and worldview directly affect the "how." The "where" will only matter if we proceed with all the expertise we can to recognize and deal with cultural differences.

In teamwork, silence isn't golden, it's deadly.
MARK SANBORN

Deaths and crashes are vivid reminders of something gone wrong. Wouldn't it have been fortunate if instead of restructuring due to devastating problems, structuring could have been done prior? How might this story have read if the airline had created a knowledge base and dialogue about cultural values, so that culture could operate in a way that it brought gain instead of loss?

To their credit, Korean Air, and Boeing, whose plane was involved, both acknowledged the need for and embraced an attention to cultural communication, bringing cultural training to the forefront. Keeping the attention on the "how" of their business, they set out to prevent culture from being a hindrance and to harness the good it can bring if understood.

Although your work may not have such vivid examples of the need to attend to culture, there most likely are some less traumatic effects of culture operating in your daily efforts. There will only be more as businesses become increasingly more global.

Diversity is the mix. Inclusion is getting the mix to work.

YOUR INVISIBLE TOOLBOX

Are you "structuring" by gaining the knowledge and skills about diversity and inclusion on teams that are available so you won't have to publicly "restructure" when it comes to culture?

Dialogue cultural values

52

THE EVERYDAY DIPLOMAT

*I think there are probably two things we can look for as millennials
take over. The first is the likelihood of looking for cooperative solutions
internationally. Millennials score higher on various cooperation indices
(so) I think their instinct for trying diplomacy may be first and
longer than other generations might have is something we
can look forward to over the decades.
The second thing—and it's related—is that millennials are
much less supportive of the use of force to solve problems.*
TREVOR THRALL

The hotel airport shuttle arrived at 3:45 a.m. Nine people were
gathered to board, groggy and bleary-eyed in the damp entryway of the
hotel. Clearly a group formed with only one thing in common. They had
all missed connecting flights the day before, and due to weather and scarcity
of aircrafts to their particular destinations, they were delayed overnight.

The shuttle driver loaded the luggage as they boarded the van. A
family of four climbed in and sat on the bench seat in the back, although
they looked as if they wished they could sit separately. The dad, mom,
and two teenage boys seemed resigned rather than excited. Travel delays
can do that. What might have been a fun family experience had turned
into a test of endurance when stuck overnight, off the vacation schedule,
in one cramped hotel room.

Several others appeared to be business travelers, for the dim interior
light of the van illuminated rather wrinkled and tired-looking business
suits and faces. A young backpacking couple took the seat in front. The
young man carefully handed his wife a glass jar to hold as they sat down.
In the jar was the fragile cut of a plant they must have found while on
vacation and wanted to root at home.

The wait was cold and uncomfortable. The energy on the bus was one of mild impatience. No one wanted to miss their earliest opportunity to get home. Why wasn't the van moving?

The young man in front wiped the condensation off the window to see what the delay was. The driver was talking to a woman who was trying to get organized to board the bus. She had a lot of bags and appeared to have difficulty walking. Her ankles protruding over her shoes gave her a faulty gait. Her size prevented her from carrying her bags surely, and one had dropped. The commotion and delay triggered a definite feeling of exasperation for the waiting passengers. Wrapped in individual discontent, they seemed unable to move. It was as if they had all silently agreed to just endure the situation and layer their ill will this woman's circumstance and the delay brought right on top of their feelings of fatigue, cold, and discontent. The bad feeling in the van was as tangible as the uncomfortable seats.

Right at this moment, the young man with the plant asked his wife, "Do you mind if I help?"

She whispered back, "No, please do."

He got up and quickly descended the van steps. "Good morning, can I help you?" he cheerily addressed the woman who was causing the delay. They talked for a moment, and then up the steps he came, securing her carry-on bag under the seat before quickly descending again to take her arm and carefully help her up. He made sure she was seated comfortably, made eye contact, and asked quietly if there was anything else he could do. The dim light of the van seemed to brighten as he smiled at her.

The young man sat down. The driver, who due to this man's help had time to finish loading the bags, boarded and started the van. The man seated directly behind the woman spoke to her, as if continuing the help he had observed, engaging her in a conversation about her destination. The dark mood had lifted. The spell was broken.

Instead of joining in on the prevailing bad mood, allowing her to climb into the bus feeling awkward and late at the expense of fellow travelers, the man with the plant diplomatically, tactfully took care of her and everyone else.

Diplomacy is more than saying or doing the right things at the right time,
it is avoiding saying or doing the wrong things at any time.
BO BENNETT

How many times in life do we fail to exercise diplomacy due to our surroundings? Maybe it's not what the people around us do; maybe it's not how people act in the culture of our workplace. Maybe it's too much effort.

Yet to observe an individual choosing to act in a way that tactfully and surely makes it better for everybody is an amazing thing. Not unlike seeing someone taking the time and care to bring a plant cutting home to remember things by.

Diplomacy: it may be at its best found in the everyday.

YOUR INVISIBLE TOOLBOX

Diplomacy is not saved for those in government. By acting in a diplomatic way and attending to situations with tact and understanding, you yield dividends in work environments. What action could you take to diplomatically assist either someone or a situation in order to make it go more smoothly for all?

Act with diplomacy

Part IV

TOOLS FOR LEADERS

The fascination with millennials has led to the publication of a staggering number of books, articles, and training programs designed to understand the members of this new largest generation to enter the workforce and provide guidance on how to lead them.

What about when the tables shift and the millennials are called upon to lead?

While there are exemplary examples of millennial entrepreneurs and an increasing number of millennials climbing through corporate ranks, the data is still too scarce to say anything definitively about this group and their unique leadership philosophies, capabilities, and blind spots.

What we do know is that millennials will be called to lead in organizations where the pace of change is breathtaking. As leaders, they will be faced with challenges they've never seen in the past and no leaders that preceded them have dealt with. The ability to acquire leadership skills through experience or from mentors who have "walked in their shoes" will be profoundly insufficient.

In this part of the book, we examine the tools for leading others.

A true leader has the confidence to stand alone, the courage to
make tough decisions, and the compassion to listen to the needs of others.
He does not set out to be a leader, but becomes one by the equality
of his actions and the integrity of his intent.
DOUGLAS MACARTHUR

53

THE SHOULDERS OF GIANTS

One of the traits about millennials in least dispute is their belief that working in collaboration with others and being part of a team are keys for fostering an inspiring workplace and achieving business success.

This core understanding that people rarely achieve greatness alone and that the contributions of people can be combined for success will serve millennials well in their careers. It may be one of the most valued qualities millennials bring to the interconnected work environments that characterize modern organizations.

Do they also hold the same reverence for the teams who came before them and achieved the successes that the workers of the future can build upon?

The new school year had just begun at Robinson High School in Little Rock, Arkansas. Martha Cothren, a social studies teacher, taught her students a powerful lesson on that day in September 2005 when they arrived to school to find there were no desks in the classroom.

When the students inquired about their desks, she said, "You can't have a desk until you tell me how you earn them."

The young people pondered the question and came up with a few ideas. Some wondered if they earned the desks by getting good grades. Some speculated that they might earn them with good behavior. She told them that was not how they earned the desks.

By early afternoon news of this unusual experiment had spread. A television crew arrived to report on the crazy teacher who had taken the desks away. Finally the last period came and no one had figured out how they earned their desk. She invited the students to sit around the edges of the room on the floor so she could tell them.

She opened the door to the classroom and welcomed twenty-seven US military veterans, wearing their uniforms, to the classroom. Each veteran was carrying a desk. They placed the desks in rows and then stood by the walls.

The students had their aha moment. They were beginning to understand how the desks were earned. Ms. Cothren said, "You don't have to earn those desks. These guys did it for you. They put them out there for you, but it's up to you to sit here responsibly to learn, to be good students and good citizens, because they paid a price for you to have that desk, and don't ever forget it."

> *If I have seen further than others, it is by standing*
> *upon the shoulders of giants.*
> ISAAC NEWTON

In 2006 the Veterans of Foreign Wars named Martha Cothren as their "Teacher of the Year."

The generations that came before us have made important contributions to the world we live in now. The leaders and employees who came before us have made important contributions to the organizations we work in now and have the opportunity to serve.

YOUR INVISIBLE TOOLBOX

Your own success is built upon the efforts of those who came before you.

Recognize past contributions

54

RIGHTING A WRONG

Millennials say putting people first, acting with integrity, and living by a code of ethics are key factors contributing to long-term success. They extend that attitude to organizations. In choosing an employer, they favor companies that share their values. As consumers, they are willing to pay a premium for products and services provided by companies with strong corporate social responsibility reputations. Their employment and buying patterns confirm this. It would seem that millennials put their decisions where their mouths are.

It's easy to do right when choices are clear. What happens when situations are more complex, when values collide, or when mistakes happen? What do you do then? Do you stand by your principles? How do you handle your mistakes? What do you do when you discover a mistake made by someone else? We'd all like to think that we would call attention to the error and make amends. Do we? Do you?

"I have no anger towards Judge Aspen at all. ... He wrote a beautiful letter for me to the president of the United States. It means a whole lot to me, that letting me know that he was giving me the opportunity that he couldn't have gave me the first time, this time. I would actually thank him for giving me a second chance at life."

Alton Mills made these remarks when asked to comment about the US federal judge who had sentenced him to a mandatory life sentence in prison for federal cocaine violations. After serving twenty-two years, President Barack Obama commuted his life sentence.

Congress enacted sentencing laws that dramatically increased penalties for drug crimes in response to rising public concern about high crime rates in the 1980s and 1990s. The laws, intended to improve public safety, did not deliver those results, as the availability and use of illegal drugs increased and recidivism rates remained largely unchanged.

What did happen was the mandatory minimum sentences for drug possession resulted in thousands of low-level drug offenders serving more time in federal prisons for minor drug offenses than they would have for violent crimes like bank robbery, rape, or even murder. Alton Mills was one example. The more serious drug traffickers, who were the focus of the laws, were largely unaffected.

What lessons can we learn from this story? There are two insights:

1. Leaders make mistakes. Leadership decisions, even those that are well-intentioned, sometimes have unintended negative consequences. When leaders discover a mistake, even one they didn't personally make, they are faced with an important choice. What do I do next? How do I correct the mistake? Federal Judge Marvin Aspen wrote to Obama, asking him to grant clemency to an inmate whose sentence did not match the crime.

2. People make mistakes. The low-level drug offenders who received the harsh sentences had knowingly committed a crime. They also faced an important choice. What do I do next? How do I correct the mistake? Alton Mills is committed to making the most of his second chance and proving to the president who granted him clemency that he was worthy of it.

This chapter opened with Alton Mills responding to the question, "What would you say to the judge who sentenced you?" We'll close with the response Judge Aspen provided when asked, "What would you say to Alton Mills?"

"I would say to him that I hope he can leave prison and have a positive attitude. I know that is difficult after all he's been through. So many people have been concerned about him. I hope he can be a positive example to show that not only was a terrible mistake and injustice done to him, but that he can prove by the rest of his life that he was a worthwhile person and justify the confidence that all the people had in him, including myself."

We all make mistakes. Our true character is revealed in what we do about a mistake.

YOUR INVISIBLE TOOLBOX

Take a moment to reflect on the mistakes you have made or discovered. What can you do to right the mistake—even many years later?

Make it right

55

CLEAN YOUR ROOM

Clean your room. Please, clean your room. I'll pay you to clean your room. You can't go out until you clean your room...

Rewards, punishments, begging, nagging. Why is it so challenging to get people to do things?

Delegation, whether at work or at home, is an area where many leaders struggle. Many times it seems simpler and more expedient to do the work themselves.

No man will make a great leader who wants to do it all himself
or get all the credit for doing it.
ANDREW CARNEGIE

When done well, delegation benefits everyone. Leaders free up time for other activities. Followers grow and contribute. Organizations achieve more. Many of us have never learned how to delegate well, and we stress over whether the delegated task will get done right, or at all. Here are some fast tips.

Leaders must correctly diagnose two areas: skills and interest. If someone knows how to do the task and likes it, delegation is appropriate. If one of those two variables is lacking, a different leadership action is needed.

Skills and Knowledge

Leaders often make too many assumptions about what people can do and what they know (or should know). A decision on whether or not to delegate is further complicated by employees who underestimate the task or overestimate their own skills and abilities. When someone lacks skills or knowledge in any measure, delegation is risky.

Let's return to the "clean your room" example. Parents commonly believe that their young ones already possess the necessary skills for this job. Do they? Really?

Why would a young person know how to clean a room well? Why would he or she share the same definition of "clean" that a parent does? If you've ever been met with the response "I did clean it" and the result didn't meet your standards, chances are there was a skill or knowledge gap. Delegation wasn't appropriate.

Interest and Motivation

If people have the skills and knowledge, can the leader delegate? It depends. Do they also possess sufficient interest and motivation?

All of us must do things we're skilled at but lack interest in. We procrastinate. We make excuses. If we find the task itself motivating, then delegation is appropriate. If not, delegation may fail. You may find this true of the exercise program you keep delegating yourself to do. You know what to do—you just don't want to do it.

YOUR INVISIBLE TOOLBOX

It's often hard to relinquish control. Others may not do it your way. Many times it seems more expedient (and simpler) to do the work yourself. Rather than learning to delegate effectively, you work longer hours. To improve the chances of success, leaders must diagnose a follower's readiness by assessing skills and motivation prior to making a decision if delegation is appropriate.

Diagnose before delegating

56

THE HEART IS WHERE THE ENTHUSIASM IS

Passionate people tend to outperform individuals with greater technical qualifications or skills. Without passion, individuals can lose their knowledge advantage through complacency. Leaders who match individuals to jobs they are not only skilled in but also feel motivated to do will thrive in the face of today's rapid changes.

A common approach to motivating people is to reward them for the behaviors leaders want to see and punish those they don't want to see. Hence the common saying, "What gets rewarded gets done."

Motivation theorist Frederick Herzberg describes external rewards like pay and benefits as hygiene factors. They are like temperature. When the room temperature is comfortable, we don't think about it. When it's too hot or cold, we're unhappy and think about little else. Similarly, the absence of rewards can be demotivating. The presence of rewards is not, in isolation, motivating.

It is very tricky to use external motivation because managers have such a hard time finding a reward with value to the employee. It takes a manager who knows an individual very personally to find an external motivation with value, and then one that won't offend the other employees.

Employee motivation can consume management. I like to focus less on the right formula for amounts of external motivation, and more on creating a culture where internal motivation is grown. To me it comes down to the 'teaching to fish' parable. I can 'give a fish' to an employee, or I can teach them to 'get fish' on their own. I have found that spending time creating a culture where individuals see personal success and team success helps drive internal motivation.
STEPHEN VALBRACHT

Inner motivation is something that motivates people to want to do something without expecting a reward. According to study after study, people report feeling motivated by things like: making a difference, a sense of accomplishment, pride in good work, sense of growth, being challenged, and working with great colleagues. These elements of inner motivation transcend generations, genders, and cultures. Apparently they are fundamentally timeless human characteristics.

If we don't tap into the emotion and passion of others, we are unlikely to achieve much more than short-term, limited success. Competent leaders do not underestimate this challenge. They know they cannot force someone to be passionate, and they understand the difference between external and internal motivation. They devote energy to creating an environment that fosters and naturally promotes inner motivation.

Does this mean leaders shouldn't reward people? Rewards are important when they're given as recognition rather than bribe. When rewards recognize the intrinsic motivation already in play, people cherish them for what they symbolize.

Stephen Covey, author of the seminal book *The Seven Habits of Highly Effective People*, once said, "You can buy a person's hand, but you can't buy his heart. You can buy his back, but you can't buy his brain. His heart is where his enthusiasm is; his brain is where his creativity is, his ingenuity, his resourcefulness."

YOUR INVISIBLE TOOLBOX

If you're frustrated that you can't offer greater rewards to your team, reflect on the tireless efforts that people devote in the spirit of volunteerism and ask yourself why. You'll probably reach the same conclusion the motivation studies report. Tapping inner motivation doesn't require a larger budget. It requires leadership.

Tap internal motivation

57

ENOUGH HELPING HANDS

Millennials are often celebrated for their community-mindedness and civic engagement. Conversely, they are also criticized for caring little about anything but themselves. Which view is correct? Perhaps they both are. Is it possible that millennials' sense of self-importance is derived from doing good work and contributing to social causes?

The correct answer is impossible to know at the time of this writing. The ability to look at situations in hindsight provides greater accuracy. That is something that won't be available to us until millennials have lived long enough to make their mark on the world as a cohort. For now, the long-term contributions millennials will make to community, government, the environment, and the planet will remain mysteries.

What we do know is that millennials' fascination and proficiency with technology has ushered in a new age of getting things done by community. Enter crowd sourcing. Crowd sourcing (a combination of the words "crowd" and "outsourcing") is the act of bringing people together to get work done or raise money for a common interest. The results are impressive, with the most famous example being Wikipedia, the free online encyclopedia written collaboratively by the people who use it.

Every day for four years Josh Cyganik waved to Leonard Bullock, the seventy-five-year-old retired forklift driver who enjoyed sitting on his porch at his home in Pendleton, Oregon. The house was located across from where Josh worked maintaining tracks for Union Pacific's western region.

One day Josh overheard some kids making rude remarks about Leonard's home and how it was in such bad shape that it should be burned to the ground. He was touched with deep compassion when he saw the hurt in Leonard's face and realized he too had heard these words.

After stewing over the incident for a couple of days, Josh decided to try to create something positive. He asked permission to paint Leonard's house. When his offer was accepted enthusiastically, Josh leapt into action. He enlisted a friend who managed a lumber store to donate supplies and recruited coworkers to paint the house. Even with the team he had assembled, Josh was worried that he wouldn't have enough helping hands. He made a Facebook post pleading for more volunteers. The post went viral.

The next week more than one hundred people showed up to help paint. Others sent in donations of money, food, and drinks. Starbucks provided water and iced tea.

From one man's act of kindness, many came together to help a stranger. Not only did the house get painted, but construction of a new deck followed, with other projects not far behind. Leonard and his wife, Dorothy, are reported to be so delighted that they sit on the porch in the dark enjoying the beautiful home improvements they were never able to afford on their fixed income.

"According to the media, I'm a hero. I'm not a hero; I just heard something that bothered me," Josh Cyganik said. "Anyone would have done the same thing. Everyone has it in their heart to do things like this." Is he right?

Most leadership happens on a small scale in everyday situations. Wise leaders know that they need to start small with recognizable, feasible steps toward the larger goal. Tackling the whole thing at once would be too overwhelming.

I've found that small wins, small projects, small differences
often make huge differences.
ROSABETH MOSS KANTER

YOUR INVISIBLE TOOLBOX

The small, doable steps are called small wins, and they are imperative for fueling the positive momentum toward the final goal.

Start with small wins

58

WHAT IF I CAN'T MAKE A DIFFERENCE?

Decision-making falls to every individual in the workplace, one way or another. Millennials who work well in teams, show motivation to have an impact on their organizations, and desire open and frequent communication with leaders provide a wonderful climate for good decision-making.

Yet how many extremely important decisions are made every day in organizations that aren't good? How many are poorly communicated or lack the ability to influence through collaboration and result in less than desirable outcomes? How many times is only one party willing to work collaboratively? How often are decisions made that consider only short-term results at the expense of long-term consequences?

There are many reasons the story of the space shuttle *Challenger* is a tragic one. The United States lost seven high-performing individuals. Their families suffered the irreparable loss of their loved ones. The US space program and NASA were set back, and some have said the shuttle program never fully recovered from the event. What happened?

At Cape Canaveral, Florida, on January 28, 1986, the space shuttle *Challenger* broke apart and disintegrated minutes after takeoff. A much publicized launch, this shuttle carried not only five astronauts but two payload specialists, one a teacher named Christa McAuliffe, who had won the seat to be the first teacher in space over eleven thousand applicants. Though her name is well known, what is little known to most about this disaster is that it was preventable and actually roots back to communication the day before the flight.

As we reflect back upon the tragic loss of Challenger and her brave crew
of heroes who were aboard that fateful day, I am reminded that they truly
represented the best of us, as they climbed aloft on a plume of propellant
gasses, reaching for the stars, to inspire us who were Earthbound.
BUZZ ALDRIN

Bob Ebeling, who died in 2016 at eighty-nine, was one of the engineers the *New York Times* obituary stated "knew what the rest of the world did not." Ebeling predicted the fate of the *Challenger* the day before the launch. As an engineer for Thiokol, the contractor responsible for the rubber O rings designed to seal joints between the booster rocket segments, Ebeling knew these rings didn't perform well in cold weather.

On the day of the disaster, Florida was suffering a cold snap that made liftoff temperatures thirty degrees lower than any prior test launch. The O rings were not created to function in such low temperatures, and Ebeling told his daughter on the way to watch the launch at his company headquarters in Utah that the *Challenger* was going to blow up due to the cold and that everyone was going to die. That's precisely what happened.

The afternoon and evening prior to the launch, knowing the temperature would be even colder overnight, Bob Ebeling alerted his managers, and the engineers at Thiokol quickly got on the phone with NASA, trying to influence the decision to postpone the launch. They were not successful, and the outcome due to weather and the function of the rings played out as Ebeling had predicted and the Thiokol management had warned.

Why are we relating this story? The Rogers Commission found NASA's organizational culture and decision-making processes key contributing factors to the accident. You have to wonder if this situation would have been different if the decision could have been better influenced through the communications on those conference calls. You also wonder if the organizational culture and decision-making processes could have benefitted from some skills around collaboration to achieve the best possible outcomes. Or if the long-term effects were sufficiently considered, not just the short-term decision to launch or not launch on that given day.

Bob Ebeling, who was interviewed by NPR on the thirty-year anniversary of the disaster just months before he died, said he had been under terrible stress for all the years after it happened. He had bad dreams and headaches and felt like a loser because he wasn't able to prevent it. Though he was a skilled engineer who graduated from California Polytechnic University, he left the profession of engineering shortly after the *Challenger* disaster.

When others who held more responsibility than Ebeling heard the NPR interview, they reached out to him to reassure him he was not at fault. "He was not a loser, he did do something," said Allan McDonald, Ebeling's supervisor at the time. "If he hadn't called me, we never would have had the opportunity to try to avert the disaster."

Bob Ebeling was said to have appreciated these comments, so he did put his feeling of responsibility to rest before he was laid to rest. But this event had affected him until the very end of his life.

What can we learn from this account?

Of all the skills humans possess, the ability to communicate in ways that influence outcomes for everyone's best interest is one of the most significant. Organizational decision-making that requires the skills of collaborative communication and influencing, even if we're not the ones in authority, are best learned, practiced, and established before we are faced with a critical situation. "At least we had the opportunity to try to stop it," McDonald was quoted as saying. If only they would have known how to make the difference.

YOUR INVISIBLE TOOLBOX

Ask open-ended questions to get people to think and talk about the long-term interests rather than the short-term issue. This is a key skill of collaboration.

Ask open-ended questions

59

THE LEADER'S LYRICS

Have you ever been driving down the road and found yourself singing along with the tune playing on your device? Do you sometimes wonder how many times you heard the song before you memorized the words and could sing them with enthusiasm and passion, mimicking (probably poorly) the artist?

In most cases, the first few times we hear a song, it doesn't even register on a conscious level. Sometime later, perhaps when our minds are clear, void of distractions, and generally at peace, the song reaches our conscious. At that time, we make a decision about how we feel about the song.

After hearing the song a few more times, we begin to connect with it. The rhythm moves us. The chorus becomes familiar. Before we know it, we can sing along. Even then, without the music in the background, we probably can't recall the words. We may only remember the general theme of the song, how it makes us feel, and the artist's name. Therein lies some great insight for leaders.

Any idea, plan, or purpose may be placed in the mind through repetition of thought.
NAPOLEON HILL

We carefully craft our important messages, giving a great deal of thought to how our audience will receive them, only to have most of them remember very little if any of our words, much like the first time we hear a new song.

So how do we make sure others leave us singing our song? Especially when the lyrics are completely new?

Think about the mood people are in when they listen to your message. Ask yourself if there's anything you can do to create a mental state in your listeners that primes them for your message.

YOUR INVISIBLE TOOLBOX

As you prepare your messages, you can learn from the great songwriters to develop a catchy chorus and use it frequently throughout your communications. How many times did you need to hear the song before you could recite the lyrics? How many times did you hear the song before you were conscious that you even heard the song? These are interesting questions and food for thought for leaders.

Use repetition in communication

60

DO YOU LOOK HONEST?

Ninety-one percent of millennials aspire to be leaders. What kind of leader do millennials say they want to be? Ones who strive to empower others, plan to use a collaborative leadership style, seek to lead with purpose, desire to give back to society, and do meaningful work.

How is success against those leadership goals measured?

In many tangible tasks and activities, performance can be quickly assessed. A professional creating a new spreadsheet, for example, can receive immediate feedback by looking at the results. This helps inform what adjustments can be made for the next one.

But most leadership activities are different. Leadership is rarely a repetitive behavior and is never a solitary activity. By definition, leadership is about people. In their classic leadership text, *The Leadership Challenge*, authors James Kouzes and Barry Posner present research about which behaviors followers consider most important in their leaders. Survey respondents cited four characteristics over 50 percent of the time.

- Honesty
- Forward-looking
- Inspiring
- Competent

Unlike creating a spreadsheet, these qualities are largely intangible, and success can only be assessed over time.

It's not what we do once in a while that shapes our lives.
It's what we do consistently.
TONY ROBBINS

So how are you performing as a leader? Some of the only data available to people entrusted to your leadership on a daily basis is how you look and sound. Your pace when you walk into a room, the eye contact you make with others, your hand movements, facial expression, and vocal quality all communicate nonverbally—for better or worse. These behaviors shape the perceptions others hold of you.

Appearances matter. Do a self-audit. How are you perceived?

Is your body language and vocal quality communicating that you're honest, forward-thinking, inspiring, and competent? Or do you, like many busy people, unintentionally and nonverbally communicate qualities such as impatience, disinterest, insecurity, incapability, or uncertainty?

How do you know if you're performing well in areas that don't allow for immediate feedback?

Long term, your legacy will ultimately confirm your leadership performance. In the short term, exemplary leaders realize that influencing the perceptions others hold of them as they exercise leadership is critical.

YOUR INVISIBLE TOOLBOX

Do you look honest? Do you come across as confident, competent, and inspiring? Can people tell you are forward-thinking?

Conduct a self-audit

61

NOT THE TRUSTING TYPE

According to polling by Harvard University's Institute of Politics, millennials trust only two major societal institutions, the military and scientists. Members of the millennial generation are skeptical of others, especially the media, Wall Street, and Congress. What implications will that have on their success?

Do you trust until you have a reason not to?

Presumption of innocence is a fundamental right in most civilized countries. In criminal trials, the burden of proof rests on the prosecution, which is required to meet a threshold of presenting evidence to convince beyond a reasonable doubt. So indoctrinated are we to that concept that a presumption of guilt is regarded as immoral. To that end, business practices such as pre-employment drug testing are frequently the target of rights activists who believe they violate the principle by requiring job candidates to prove themselves innocent.

Beyond law and order, the presumption of innocence has implications in all aspects of our lives. From parenting to education to business to politics and everything in between, we are continuously challenged to assume the best in others and suffer the disappointment and consequences when our trust turns out to have been misplaced.

In the business world, leaders are encouraged to build a culture of trust. Evidence of this consistent message to leaders was revealed through a casual Google search on the words "trust" and "leadership" that yielded over 350 million hits. Nearly all of the books, articles, classes, and speeches on the subject extol the virtues of trust, remind leaders that employee surveys reveal a deficit of trust, and encourage leaders to trust more and assume the best. After all, presuming innocence is not only an essential moral foundation of a civilized society, it is also sensible business practice.

Or is it?

Consider these statistics from the 2012 Josephson Institute Report Card on the Ethics of American Youth. The Josephson Institute of Ethics administers the CHARACTER COUNTS! youth ethics project, and their survey of 23,000 young people asked questions about their behavior in the past twelve months. These are the findings:

- 76 percent admit they lied to a parent about something significant, while 55 percent admit they lied to a teacher.
- 51 percent admit to cheating during a test at school.
- 32 percent admit to copying an Internet document.
- 20 percent admit to stealing something from a store, 18 percent stole from a parent or relative, and 14 percent stole from a friend.

How did the survey respondents feel about their own behavior?

- 99 percent said "it's important for me to be a person with good character."
- 93 percent report that they are "satisfied with my own ethics and character."
- 81 percent responded that "when it comes to doing what's right, I'm better than most people I know."

The numbers tell an interesting story. The same people who describe themselves as ethical also admitted to lying, cheating, and stealing...on the same survey.

What can be gleaned from these contradictions? Apparently the behaviors of lying, cheating, and stealing that the survey respondents admitted to have been justified in their own minds, extending to themselves the presumption of innocence.

It's a disturbing thought that the young people who confessed to these ethical breaches today are the parents, educators, colleagues, employees, leaders, elected officials, and business owners of tomorrow.

It's difficult to find leaders at any level who don't readily agree about the importance of honesty and trust. However, the same leaders, like the young people surveyed, frequently fall short when called upon to translate the virtue they embrace into action. Is it any surprise that millennials are cynical when it comes to societal institutions?

Is there a solution? Can a trusting nature and a healthy dose of skepticism coexist in organizations? Can a culture of trust be fostered at the same time as a culture that challenges the choices people make? The questions are troubling and the actions called for unclear. For leaders charged with building a culture of trust in organizations, the complexity of nurturing an ethical environment can be overwhelming.

YOUR INVISIBLE TOOLBOX

Remind yourself that the presumption of innocence afforded to an individual does not require naiveté when considering large numbers of people that surveys reveal bend rules and later rationalize their own bad behavior. Assume the best in others while also championing the establishment of safeguards to reduce both temptation and the ease of wrongdoing by individuals inclined to breach ethics.

Champion safeguards

62

A SIGN OF A HEALTHY, ACTIVE BRAIN

"You can't be too careful." That could be the motto of the millennial generation whose lives have been shaped by helicopter parents on a mission to prevent bad things from happening, the age of terrorism, and a media culture constantly focusing on negative events and highlighting dangers.

A Better Business Bureau survey revealed that contrary to widely held beliefs that seniors are at greatest risk of being prey to fraudsters, millennials are more likely to be scammed than their elders. And the problem is more widespread than you may think.

According to researchers Victoria Talwar and Kang Lee, children start telling lies to conceal wrongdoings around the age of two. By age four, the lies are more complex. As children continue to mature, so do their cognitive abilities and lie-telling skills. Around age seven, the lies become more creative. Lying is a sign of a healthy, active brain. After all, keeping lies straight requires a lot of mental abilities.

From seemingly harmless white lies to complex cover-ups and major deceptions, lying seems to be a core part of human nature. It is something the business professional must deal with proactively or face the consequences of being misled.

The glue that holds all relationships together—including the relationship between the leader and the led—is trust, and trust is based on integrity.
BRIAN TRACY

How do we protect ourselves from con artists? Can we spot liars and safeguard our reputation and possessions? Deception is difficult to detect. We like to think we can tell if we're being deceived, but the facts prove differently. Efforts by people to accurately diagnose deception have been undependable, even by judges and police officers who get a lot of practice with being lied to. Similarly, polygraph tests have proven unreliable in detecting lies and provide a disturbing number of false positives.

YOUR INVISIBLE TOOLBOX

Trust and also verify. Ask for details. Ask for information to be repeated. Ask lots of questions about different topics. Ask for written summaries of steps taken and actions agreed. Even the most skilled liars will often stumble when required to fabricate many answers or record their deeds on paper.

Trust and verify

63

CREDIBILITY CHECK

The reasons cited for an interest in leadership by millennials are stirring. Far beyond meeting bottom-line goals, they hope to make a difference in the world. They want to inspire and empower others. Only 5 percent say they are interested in leadership for the money.

So you're thinking about becoming a leader. While having ambitious and lofty goals is admirable, when it comes to leadership, your own opinion of your ability doesn't matter much. What matters most is the perception of others.

Leadership is a reciprocal relationship between those who accept the challenge to lead and those who choose to follow. Any discussion of leadership must attend to the dynamics of that relationship. Strategies, tactics, skills, and best practices are empty unless you understand the fundamental human aspirations that connect leaders and their followers.

When we get a loan or apply for a credit card, a credit check is done. The reason for this is to see if the lender or credit card company can trust or believe us. The root word for credibility is "credo," which means I trust or I believe. It is the same root word for credit.

Followers too want to know that they can trust their leaders.

I think it's very important to have a feedback loop, where you're constantly thinking about what you've done and how you could be doing it better. I think that's the single best piece of advice: constantly think about how you could be doing things better and questioning yourself.
ELON MUSK

YOUR INVISIBLE TOOLBOX

How can you build your credibility? By becoming the rare leader who carefully and consciously chooses your behavior and seeks feedback. Solicit a credit report in the form of a 360-degree leadership assessment. This informs how your leadership behaviors are perceived by others.

Solicit feedback

—————————— 64 ——————————

IN PERSON OR IN WRITING

When asked to describe themselves, millennials cite technology as the most defining characteristic of their generation. They also say that they prefer texting over phone conversations. Most of them admit to sleeping with their devices next to them, to checking them when attending live events such as concerts or shows, and using them on the toilet.

Are today's devices a good substitute for interactions in the workplace? Or is modern technology causing millennials to lose their ability to interact with each other? Will this and future generations of workers possess sufficient interpersonal skills and knowledge to make real the claim that leaders proudly make "people are our most valuable asset"?

When is e-communication appropriate and when is face-to-face interaction superior?

Think about occasions when leaders have to deliver bad news. Leaders frequently must provide feedback to employees around negative performances. Even sharing disappointing news that is less personal can be hard, such as telling your customer you can't meet their demands.

When delivering bad news, you should make the effort to deliver it face-to-face or during a personal phone call if an in-person meeting isn't possible. Why? Receiving bad news is hard for people. The opportunity for eye contact and a discussion can make the interaction more productive. Most millennials find delivering bad news or critique difficult, so they hide behind their devices.

This is important for millennials who are at the heart of the growing trend of dumping someone in a romantic relationship digitally. Not only can it be perceived as a demonstration of cowardice on the part of the individual doing the breaking up, it is creating an unfortunate habit that won't serve us well in the workplace where we are expected to be able to talk to one another.

Electric communication will never be a substitute for the face of someone who with their soul encourages another person to be brave and true.
CHARLES DICKENS

What about good news? When you're offering a compliment or extending thanks, written communication is worthy of consideration. Why? Because a written record of good news is something that can be revisited. It's common for people to save and treasure thoughtful handwritten notes for years. Electronic forms of written communication easily allow you to copy others on the message and share the good news more broadly, which can help to improve morale and tap inner motivation.

If you have something nice to say, put it in writing. If you have something challenging to communicate, do it in person.

YOUR INVISIBLE TOOLBOX

While technology may make for expedient routine communication, it is a poor substitute for the human connections that people crave.

Deliver bad news in person

65

LOOK...A SQUIRREL

What is the attention span of a millennial?

Hint: it's the same as other generations and shorter than a goldfish's.

It is eight seconds.

You probably didn't even notice, but the first three lines of this chapter used three classic audience engagement techniques that you can employ in your communications as a leader to quickly engage your listeners.

Asking the question, "What is the attention span of a millennial?" quickly gets people involved in the communication and helps them remember. It has been estimated that people remember more than 85 percent of the questions they are asked and fewer than 30 percent of the sentences they hear. When you use questions, even rhetorical ones, you can get people thinking, surprise them, encourage involvement, or invite agreement.

Following up the question was this analogy: "Hint: it's the same as other generations and shorter than a goldfish's." Analogies compare a point you are making to something that is familiar to your audience. Using analogies, you can get your point across more effectively and in less time. Analogies are especially useful when your subject is complex. When used well, people may remember your analogy forever.

Last, we gave you a statistic: eight seconds! When you introduce a startling statistic, you shock your listeners and prove your point. A word of caution: using too many numbers or complex statistics when communicating a message can result in quickly losing an audience.

In "Hamilton," we're telling the stories of old, dead white men, but we're using actors of color, and that makes the story more immediate and more accessible to a contemporary audience.

LIN-MANUEL MIRANDA

Questions, analogies, and statistics peppered throughout your communication grab attention and keep listeners with you. But grabbing attention isn't the only concern when communicating in a leadership role. Here are two additional engagement techniques to help bridge the gap between you as a leader and your listeners to make sure they value your message. Try sharing the inside "scoop" or a story.

Leaders can get people to engage and partner with them if they can share an inside scoop. When leaders share the inside scoop concerning a change or an event, they not only have everyone's attention, they also elicit trust. People like to be "in the know," and the inside scoop unites them with your message rather than just receiving the information.

You can also elicit trust and buy-in for ideas by telling a compelling story to support your point. Sharing your own personal experiences related to the topic invites the people you lead to see you as a person. Stories are also an engagement opportunity to connect your experiences to your listeners' experiences.

Attention spans are dropping. Texts. E-mails. Social media. YouTube. These are just a few of the distractions that leaders face in the modern workplace. Leadership roles are less formal and not always based on authority or position that would demand people engage with and value what you say.

How can you get your message received in meetings? How can you keep people engaged in a topic? How can you help people focus and value what you have to say?

YOUR INVISIBLE TOOLBOX

Keeping people engaged is becoming increasingly difficult with all the distractions competing for attention. Eliciting value for what you say may be challenging. Strategically using attention-getting techniques increases the chance that your communications will be received and acted upon.

Keep people engaged

66

LESSONS FROM ELEVATOR SCHOOL

How do you feel about someone who boards the elevator, faces you, and talks? Uncomfortable. Clearly they have not been to elevator school.

Let's refresh your memory: When you're waiting for the elevator, it's permissible to talk. When the elevator arrives, you board, push the button for your floor, go to the back of the elevator (corner if available), and silently watch the floor numbers.

Everyone knows that the only time it's permissible to talk on an elevator is when there are only two people or if they love each other a lot.

In America, we protect a personal distance around us of eighteen inches. The distance varies by culture. We don't allow anyone in our personal space unless we love them a lot or we're going to hit them. This space is violated on an elevator, and that's why we don't talk. It's also the reason a handshake is an excellent method of greeting someone. It allows us to make a human connection while preserving personal space.

How is this relevant to leaders?

It's amazing how many leaders set up their meeting rooms oblivious to the personal space requirements of others. Individuals who are crammed into a room are challenged to interact. They may even find it difficult to concentrate on the topic at hand. By simply providing everyone with personal space, leaders also give them think space that allows them to interact more openly and freely.

Personal space refers to an area with invisible boundaries surrounding a person's body into which intruders may not come.
ROBERT SOMMER

Try this with friends. The next time you're in a restaurant, observe how the room is set up. You're provided with about eighteen inches of table space for your stuff—plate, flatware, napkin, water glass. In the center of the table is the community space. This is for the community stuff—salt, pepper, bottle of wine.

Have fun the next time you're out for dinner by messing with the community stuff. Put the bottle of wine in your personal space and watch the reaction of your dining companions. Or crowd a member of the dinner party with the community stuff (put the salt and pepper or mashed potatoes in their personal space). This is a great way to carry out your own research in human behavior and discover how sensitive we are to personal space.

YOUR INVISIBLE TOOLBOX

The next time you lead a meeting, give some thought to room setup. Ensure everyone has at least eighteen inches of personal space on each side of them.

Provide personal space

—————————— 67 ——————————

WHY DIDN'T YOU TELL ME?

Most people don't like conflict, yet some do. Millennials are said to be interested in collaborative results rather than conflictual results.

Conflict is evident any time unproductive emotions are present. It could be anger, frustration, guilt, shame, or any emotion that works against us.

Conflict can be addressed and eradicated, but it usually takes time to unravel the events and emotions that caused it and put relationships back in place after experiencing it. Thus conflict is a time waster. It gets in the way of achieving collaborative results.

There's an even bigger time robber than conflict when it comes to interactions. Trauma. There's only a thin line between conflict and trauma.

If something is:

1. Unexpected
2. Outside the realm of normal experience
3. Causes a shift in trust

It is now not conflictual but traumatic. It takes significant time and effort to recover from trauma in the workplace.

Just as the body goes into shock after a physical trauma, so does the human psyche go into shock after the impact of a major loss.
ANNE GRANT

What could push an issue from conflict to trauma in the workplace?

Anything from workplace bullying where someone is intimidated or humiliated to news of a merger that wasn't known about, to a new employee not being given a proper onboarding or information. Even simple organizational change has a potential of trauma. The magnitude may vary depending on the individual.

Unfortunately, we forget as we become veteran employees what it feels like to experience changes in the workplace for the first time.

What can be done to avoid this? Keep these suggestions in mind.

1. If possible, let people in on information ahead of time to mitigate the news registering as unexpected.

2. Don't assume your experience is everyone's or underestimate what may be outside the realm of theirs.

3. Act in ways that consistently establish trust.

True collaborative settings harbor the abilities to prevent conflict and mitigate and reduce the occurrence of trauma. In order to create them, recognition of what can be done to avoid trauma is key.

In times of change, the chance for conflict to turn traumatic is inherent. If you don't prepare your people ahead of time and assess if they have ever experienced the same kind of change before, you risk creating trauma.

YOUR INVISIBLE TOOLBOX

To mitigate trauma, strive to communicate about changes to prevent them from being unexpected.

Communicate what's changing

——— 68 ———

HOW ARE YOU FEELING?

There is no doubt that technology has changed the way we communicate, including how emotions are shared online. A simple click, and feelings are widely shared. More than other generations, millennials have taken advantage of this method of connection. Millennials could be called the open book generation when it comes to sharing feelings and emotions online.

How about off-line? How tuned-in are you to your emotional state? How much attention do you pay to feelings when interacting with others face-to-face?

A lot of experiences in the business world exact a significant emotional toll that cannot be underestimated or ignored. The type of emotions can run the gamut from anger to sadness to confusion to denial and everything in between.

Humans aren't as good as we should be in our capacity to empathize with feelings and thoughts of others, be they humans or other animals on Earth. So maybe part of our formal education should be training in empathy. Imagine how different the world would be if, in fact, that were reading, writing, arithmetic, empathy.
NEIL DEGRASSE TYSON

When unproductive emotions surface, give yourself and others grace for feeling overwhelmed. Speak openly of the emotional element tied to experiences in the workplace and reassure people that their emotions are normal. Look for ways to make people comfortable talking about their feelings. You may have to model this by talking about your own emotional reactions. It will speak volumes when they see that you too struggle with the feelings of sadness and loss.

Take time to take care of yourself before you think it's necessary. Often, competent professionals report that they feel "fine" (and therefore not in need of pampering, decompression, or relaxation) until they reach maximum stress levels and precipitate a crisis.

YOUR INVISIBLE TOOLBOX

When interacting with others, handle emotional issues with compassion. Conflict, frustration, anger, and sadness all require a great deal of courage to share.

Handle emotions with compassion

—————————— 69 ——————————

WHY IS CHANGE SO HARD?

Growing up, millennials experienced a revolution in computers and technology, the rise of social media, a growing sense of environment awareness, an increase in school violence and mass murders, an escalation of domestic and international terrorism, multiple wars, and the election of the first black president of the United States. Each of these changes played a role in shaping the personality of the millennial generation.

Reflect on the major changes in your own life. It could be a career change, the birth of a child, the death of a loved one, marriage, divorce… Did the changes involve an element of loss?

All changes, even the most longed for, have their melancholy;
for what we leave behind us is a part of ourselves;
we must die to one life before we can enter another.
ANATOLE FRANCE

All changes, both positive and negative, begin with a loss. They first begin with letting go of the old.

William Bridges wrote about this intuitively logical notion in his book *Managing Transitions*. As Bridges described it, transition is the emotional process a person goes through to get from something old to something new. Before you arrive at the new location, you must leave home and travel through what Bridges calls the "Neutral Zone," which is neither home nor the intended destination.

Those leading the charge, not surprisingly, are notoriously focused on the new. They are victims of the erroneous thinking that change begins with the new. While it's tempting to think that way, this mistake is a leading cause of change failures.

In reality, or at least in emotional reality, which tends to take precedence over "objective reality," change begins with an ending.

Before we can move into the new, we must first leave the old. Leaders who fail to recognize this lead change at their peril.

Consider moving houses. This involves little more than having a moving van (or your friends and a truck) transfer your possessions from the old to the new. However, the change, as anyone who has made it knows, involves more than the physical move.

You begin with letting go of the old. Mourning the loss of the familiar. Thinking about the memories (even if they aren't fond ones). Once you actually move, things don't quickly fall into place. You wake up groggy in the middle of the night in search of a glass of water and walk into a wall because the old house didn't have a wall in that location.

You miss the old, familiar place.

You have to find a new route to work. You realize how challenging this is when one evening on your way home you unconsciously find yourself driving to the old house. You have to find a new grocery store, and the new one doesn't arrange its shelves like the old one did, so shopping takes more time.

You miss the old, familiar place.

If you made your move with a family, not only are you dealing with the process of change, you are also leading others on the journey. They miss friends and neighbors at the old location, their old school, favorite hairdresser, dry cleaner, banker, and physician.

You miss the old, familiar place.

Some people find the process of leaving the end behind so challenging that they will go to great lengths to hang onto the old. Consider people who drive a couple of hours to keep their relationship with their former hairdresser, banker, or doctor.

Even a positive change like the birth of a child requires giving up the way things were. Countless new mothers and fathers experience tremendous guilt because societal norms demand that they be euphoric at this wonderful new change. While they love the new life entrusted to their care, they also suffer in silence wondering if there is something wrong with them as they grieve the simplicity of the life left behind. Why didn't anyone tell me how hard this was going to be? Am I the only one feeling like this?

Even in the case of a planned, positive change, you miss the old, familiar place.

New processes and systems, technological advances, new teams, leaders, products, growth, downsizings, acquisitions, restructurings... like the personal changes we make, individuals in the workplace first must leave the old comfort zone behind before moving to the new.

What can you as a leader do to address this reality? Stop, pause, and dignify the ending. Celebrate where you came from and what you've achieved before running too fast into the change ahead. Mourn the past—even the parts you're happy to leave behind.

YOUR INVISIBLE TOOLBOX

Dignifying the ending is an important tradition when someone has died. It is the purpose of funerals and celebrations of life. Retirement parties are designed for the same reason. It is critical to dignify the ending before you can move into the new. Try to learn lessons on leading change by contemplating these important traditions.

Dignify the ending

70

DO YOU REMEMBER WHEN...?

Millennials, it's reported, prioritize physical assets like cars and homes less and place greater importance on personal experiences.

Experiences are nothing to be taken for granted; whether good or bad, they are firmly imprinted in the memory and can evoke significant emotions when recalled. Beyond warm memories of days past, tapping prior experiences is a useful, nontraditional leadership tool.

Recalling experiences from the past that were especially happy or heartwarming is a powerful method of imprinting people for a similar experience in the future. Athletes use this borrowing technique very effectively. They recall a victory in the past and vividly imagine repeating it in the game they are now preparing for.

When a challenging goal lies ahead, help yourself and others recall a similar experience from the past. Recall how you felt at the time. Now imagine yourself in the new situation, feeling the same way you did in the past.

The past is where you learned the lesson. The future is where you apply the lesson. Don't give up in the middle.
UNKNOWN

YOUR INVISIBLE TOOLBOX

Whenever you're faced with change and feel the need to proceed cautiously because the change could be threatening, remember how much your life improved as a result of change such as with the last new software update or the latest device. You can then imagine that the new change facing you isn't as scary as you once thought.

Borrow from the past

71

THE LAW OF THE PACK

Are millennials narcissistic and lazy, believing that they are entitled to rank and privilege they haven't earned? Or does their ambition make them anxious to leave behind what they perceive to be an outmoded framework for career growth and success?

Rank can be consciously or unconsciously assigned. Take a look at the law of the pack as it pertains to dogs.

Buster comes to his new home from a humane society shelter. As a dog, he is automatically programmed to relate to his owners as either his parents or siblings. What do his owners do? They gush over him and talk to him in a high-pitched voice that sounds to Buster more like a sibling than someone responsible for him. When he gets excited, they allow him to jump, charge through doors, drag them down the street, or claim privileges of higher rank. His position is set. He is in control. Buster outranks his owners.

What does this tell us about how each new generation is indoctrinated into the workforce?

One of the greatest challenges faced by organizations is providing a work environment and benefits that attract the best employees yet don't foster a culture of entitlement.

Entitlement and privilege corrupt.
JAMES STOCKDALE

Leaders in organizations never intend to communicate that the comfort and personal equity of the employee takes priority over what he or she is tasked to do. Yet what is the interview candidate or new employee expected to think when the tour includes a visit to a state-of-the-art fitness facility, no formal dress code, game rooms, compensated meals, convenient flex hours, and optional educational programs? Add to this the promise of lavish bonuses when the company is profitable, regardless of individual contributions.

Is there a problem with companies seeking to create a state-of-the-art workplace and exemplary employee benefits?

No. The problem lies in incomplete communication. Many organizations offer their employees a unique and upscale work experience. Zappos and Disney are two examples. What they communicate, yet many organizations fail to, are the expectations of their employees.

Zappos provides a unique organizational culture that appeals to many individuals. New employees spend several weeks in orientation being educated on the organization's goals and the expectations of each employee. Zappos is famous for "the offer," a $3,000 take it or leave it choice to stay or go after the company has outlined its expectations. Employees have the opportunity to publicly affirm that they are signing onto the expectations or they are walking.

Disney has a similarly intensive new employee orientation program that not only covers the many benefits of working for the organization but also describes the hardships employees encounter, such as unattractive shifts, strict dress codes, and the requirement to be pleasant in every situation—even when you don't feel like it.

Like Buster the dog's new owners, the intentions of the organization are good. They set out to create a wonderful experience for the new employee in the hopes that performance will follow. Instead, entitlement is the result.

What is the employee to think when amenities rather than job responsibilities are the focus of the first day walk-through? We know how Buster responded. How is the new employee going to respond?

YOUR INVISIBLE TOOLBOX

In their attempt to sell the benefits of the company, organizations often fail to put performance expectations at the forefront and help the employee see that the many benefits on offer are in exchange for top performance.

Communicate expectations

72

YOU'RE GOING TO LOVE KINDERGARTEN

Being asked for their input and seeking input from others is so much a part of the culture of millennials that the phrase "ask everyone to weigh in" could be printed on a T-shirt.

Many millennials were raised in an environment where they were invited to weigh in on decisions as routine as "what should we have for dinner?" to major decisions such as "where should we go on the family vacation?" With consulting and collaboration part of their early imprinting, most millennials when entrusted with leadership in organizations may be positioned as the generation best adapted to lead change than any previous group.

There are a lot of misconceptions surrounding change and none so pervasive or dangerous to the ultimate success of change efforts than the mistaken assumption that people resist change.

The rate of change is not going to slow down anytime soon.
If anything, competition in most industries will probably speed up
even more in the next few decades.
JOHN P. KOTTER

What would you think of parents who decided they wanted kindergarten to come as a huge surprise for their child? On the first day of kindergarten they put their son or daughter in the car and drive to the school building. They announce, "This is kindergarten. You'll like it here. You're going to learn a lot of things, and you're going to make a lot of new friends. I'll pick you up later today."

How is the child likely to react? He or she will probably throw a fit.

Parents seem to know this, so they don't surprise their little people with kindergarten. What do they do? Here are a few examples:

- They talk about it with the child. And they don't just talk about it once. They talk about it over and over again. It is a two-way dialogue and not a speech. They don't convene a family meeting and bring out a fancy PowerPoint presentation. They facilitate dialogue. They invite questions and respond.
- They share their own personal experiences on their first day of kindergarten, even though it was many years ago.
- They talk about how they feel about their little person becoming a big kid and going to kindergarten. They share the sense of loss and sadness they are experiencing as their child grows up.
- They let their little person talk to the big kids who have already gone to kindergarten (brothers, sisters, neighbors, cousins). These kids can give credible firsthand testimonials of what kindergarten is like.
- They may drive their child to the building and show him or her what kindergarten will look like. They might introduce their child to the teacher.
- They may start with preschool (kindergarten prep).
- They involve the child in decision-making where appropriate, such as shopping for clothes or school supplies.

When parents do these things, how do their children react on the first day of kindergarten?

They are excited. They are motivated. Just try to keep them home from school. They get up early, dress themselves, and anxiously anticipate the first day of the change.

This example, and thousands of similar ones, suggests that it is not change we resist. It is the unknown. Our challenge in navigating change on our own or leading others is to make the unknown more knowable.

Interestingly, leaders do not have a great track record of preparing those entrusted to their care for change. They are often accused of not caring about people, but the evidence is overwhelmingly against that theory. Leaders typically spend an extraordinary amount of time thinking about employee morale and how changes (especially major ones) will impact people. Often, they do this among their own peers, usually behind closed doors.

What they fail to do is to imprint the change early and frequently enough that people can more successfully navigate the inevitable emotions that accompany change (like parents do in preparing their child for kindergarten).

There are countless examples of employees finding out about major changes in their organizations by reading about them in the paper or hearing about them on the news.

When they do try to prepare employees for change, leaders often do it in the form of a one-time formal communication (speech during a staff meeting, carefully crafted memo or e-mail, all-employee meeting) that does little to help people process the emotions of the change they will experience or get their questions answered.

Leaders comfort themselves by calling that method "communication," but we know from our work at Tero that one-way communication is a very narrow definition. To be effective, communication must be kinesthetic, visual, and auditory. It must involve interactions, questions, and answers. When the change is a large one, communication must be frequent.

Simply telling people one time about a change does not satisfactorily prepare them to experience the change any more than announcing kindergarten in the car on the way to school is going to be the best approach.

YOUR INVISIBLE TOOLBOX

If millennials are truly collaborative in their approach to decision-making, they may be uniquely qualified to bring people along who will need to support changes or who are impacted by them.

Actively involve others

73

THE PYGMALION EFFECT

The perception of millennials as job-hoppers is pervasive. The facts are less clear as the Bureau of Labor Statistics reports that baby boomers changed jobs in their twenties at the same frequency as millennials do in their twenties. As millennials age, the truth will become clear.

In the meantime, the question of why millennials change jobs with some frequency is worth exploring.

Why does someone who has been transformed through training and on-the-job experiences provided by an organization choose to leave that organization? What can leaders do to help ensure that the individuals they invest in stay with the organization? Consider this enchanting and timeless story.

- The stakes: The training program expenses
- The characters: Professor Henry Higgins, Colonel Pickering, and Eliza Doolittle
- The wager: A language expert, Professor Henry Higgins, bets Colonel Pickering that he can take a lowly flower girl from the streets of London and pass her off as an elegant young lady of society after an intensive six-month training program.
- The tale: George Bernard Shaw wrote the classic play *Pygmalion*, which was the basis for the hit musical *My Fair Lady* and the films *Pygmalion* and *My Fair Lady*.
- The Pygmalion Effect: Pygmalion was a sculptor. According to Greek mythology, he fashioned a statue of a beautiful woman and prayed to the gods that the statue be transformed into a real woman. His wish was granted. From this mythical story came what is commonly known as the Pygmalion Effect, which states: People can be shaped by others according to how they are treated.
- The training program: Professor Higgins teaches Eliza Doolittle etiquette and protocol, shows her how to make an entrance,

dresses her as a fine lady, and transforms her cockney accent into cultured English.
• The outcome: Following her extensive training, Eliza attends a party held at Buckingham Palace and is assumed by all in attendance to be of royal heritage and is the talk of the event. Professor Higgins wins the bet.
• The rest of the story: Although Professor Higgins succeeded in transforming the flower girl, he went right on treating her like a street urchin. Eliza, speaking to Colonel Pickering, said, "You know I will always be a flower girl to Professor Higgins because he always treats me as a flower girl. But I will always be a lady to you, because you always treat me like a lady."

> *When dealing with people, remember you are not dealing with*
> *creatures of logic but creatures of emotion.*
> DALE CARNEGIE

Eliza's remarkable insight is something for all of us to ponder. In our varied roles as leaders, parents, coaches, teachers, mentors, and friends, most of us are aware of the power of the Pygmalion Effect and realize that people do indeed respond to how they are treated. To this end, we champion and provide growth opportunities for others. What we frequently forget, however, is that it is also important for us to respond to the growth individuals make and encourage others to do the same.

YOUR INVISIBLE TOOLBOX

If you remind yourself to change your treatment of others to match the changes they've made, then perhaps your employees will not feel the need to take their new skills to a new environment that is unencumbered by old expectations. Perhaps they will keep their skills and talents in the place where they grew them. And perhaps the investments you as a leader make in employee development will result in even greater returns.

Acknowledge growth

74

THE LABEL GAME

Millennials have been called the inclusion generation. They are unique from the generations that preceded them in viewing diversity as an essential ingredient for a business's competitive advantage and a critical element of a maturing civilization. As millennials enter the leadership ranks, will this view lead to a shift in how organizations operate?

We are trying to construct a more inclusive society. We are going to make a country in which no one is left out.
FRANKLIN D. ROOSEVELT

Jane Elliott was a third-grade teacher in Riceville, Iowa. Following the assassination in 1968 of Dr. Martin Luther King Jr., prominent civil rights movement leader and Nobel Peace Prize laureate, Elliott decided to teach her students about discrimination with a controversial experiment.

She segregated her students based on their eye color. The activity was designed to demonstrate the experience of being a member of a minority group. Beyond an appreciation for the experience of African Americans, the labeling activity held insightful lessons in how all people respond to how they are treated.

In the first part of the exercise, Elliott assigned the role of "superior people" to the blue-eyed students, giving them extra privileges such as a longer recess, special access to playground equipment, extra helpings at lunch, and full use of the water fountain.

So that eye color could be quickly assessed from a distance, she had the brown-eyed students wear large, visible collars around their necks. To make the case that blue-eyed people were superior, she pointed out mistakes made by brown-eyed children as evidence of their inferiority and chastised them. She highlighted and celebrated achievements of the blue-eyed children as proof that they were smarter and better people.

In the second part of the exercise she reversed the roles.

The students in each group responded to how they were treated. The "superior" students became bossy and treated the "inferior" group poorly. Their performance on tests and tasks improved significantly—beyond their previously demonstrated abilities. The "inferior" students became withdrawn and their performance on tests dropped.

The performance effect was particularly stunning as it correlated directly to how the students were treated. The blue-eyed students, when labeled inferior, were retested on the same activity they performed the previous day when they had been labeled superior. Their performance dropped markedly. The performance of the brown-eyed students on the same task improved on the second day when their label changed from inferior to superior.

The changes were immediate and profound. Within a span of minutes, the environment created by the teacher transformed the behavior of the students. A viewing of the PBS *Frontline* documentary "A Class Divided" allows viewers to observe firsthand how these children responded to how they were treated. Everyone exposed to this experience, even viewers decades later, is impacted in a significant way. It is heartbreaking to watch previously confident and outgoing children isolate themselves on the school grounds after being labeled as inferior.

Her "blue-eyes/brown-eyes" exercise is credited for making Jane Elliott famous, earning her the National Mental Health Association Award for Excellence in Education, and launching an impressive international public speaking and training career in diversity education.

Back at home, the experiment had a substantial impact on how Elliott was treated by her peer group and many members of the community. Possibly because of the young age of the students involved, the exercise did not make her popular in Riceville—at least not in the short term. After an appearance on the *Tonight Show*, teachers walked out of the teachers' lounge when Elliott arrived. Her daughter was taunted with hate messages in her junior high school.

Does an experiment involving children in Middle America in the late 1960s offer any material insight for millennials in modern organizations?

When organizations divide people into like groups, separate them from each other, and attach labels to them, they are creating an environment not dissimilar from the one Jane Elliott created for her students.

That's precisely what leaders do when they create functional areas within the business, designate work areas for various groups, and assign department labels.

- Those sales people…
- Those engineers…
- Those IT people…
- Those executives…
- Those administrative people…
- Those accountants…

It's no surprise that people in departments treat other groups within the company as if they were competitors. Name calling, stereotyping, self-promotion, and denigrating others are just a few of the common behaviors that exist when the inevitable effect of "The Label Game" is allowed to flourish.

It isn't easy to avoid the game. It makes business sense to have all the accountants working in a common area. It makes sense to have all the sales people functioning together in a sales department. Creating a laboratory environment for researchers and technicians to collaborate closely together is a good business practice. Assigning call center staff to different areas around the organization would be inefficient and confusing.

What the blue-eyes/brown-eyes experiment teaches us is labels matter. You tend to get what you expect. If we expect people to be bored, sluggish, and lazy, we will treat them that way and probably get that kind of behavior from them. If we expect them to be motivated, excited, and interested, we will treat them accordingly and probably find that they are excited and motivated.

While the research is mixed on whether or not Elliott's experiment in discrimination reduces long-term prejudice, it conclusively proves that people respond to how they are treated. A leader entrusted with the care of others is able to influence the behaviors of people interacting.

YOUR INVISIBLE TOOLBOX

Millennials may understand this more than others due to the many labels attached to their generation. Creating opportunities for mutual respect across work groups and departments aligns well with a natural orientation toward inclusivity. How inclusive are you? What value do you place on diversity in the workplace? How do you feel about working with individuals who are different from you?

Foster inclusivity

75

LET'S GET BACK TO WORK

If you had to identify, in one word, the reason why
the human race has not achieved, and never will achieve, its
full potential, that word would be meetings.
DAVE BARRY

Many meeting leaders are not equipped with the skills and knowledge to effectively facilitate a meeting. Similarly, many meeting participants contribute to the problem through their own ineffective meeting skills.

According to the Wharton Center for Applied Research at the University of Pennsylvania, the average senior executive spends twenty-three hours each week in meetings. Senior and middle managers report that a mere 56 percent of meetings are productive and that a phone call or e-mail could replace more than 25 percent of meetings.

When the resources that are involved in meetings each day are considered alongside the above statistics, the financial drain to organizations alone is devastating.

Nearly everyone in a professional environment finds themselves at some time asked to participate or present in meetings. As careers advance, increased meeting participation (and eventually meeting leadership) inevitably follows.

At all levels of organizations, individuals employ state-of-the-art process improvement methodologies to streamline activities and accomplish more with less. Curiously, and somewhat ironically, these same individuals who strive for maximum productivity in their work activities wrestle with frustration and setbacks caused by unproductive meetings.

Why are meetings unproductive?

- Lack of Progress: They are not strategically valuable. There is limited or no progress against a goal.

- Lack of Performance: They fail to bring out the best in the people who attend or those who are affected. Relationships are damaged or interpersonal friction is created.

Since meetings are simply viewed as part of business, people often don't consider the cost. Interestingly, many don't even consider meetings to be part of work. Some end with the statement, "Let's get back to work," implying that the meeting time was not work.

YOUR INVISIBLE TOOLBOX

Meeting leadership skills are some of the easiest things to change in an organization. Like most change, an investment of time in building new skills, challenging old habits, and implementing new processes is required.

Audit meeting effectiveness

—————————— 76 ——————————

GAINS IN PRODUCTIVITY

Millennials expect different things from the workplace than the generations that preceded them. They are largely unimpressed with the corner office or the usual trappings that communicate status and rank. They prefer an open work environment that fosters collaboration and provides access to decision-makers. Other appealing features to the workspace include common areas where they can enjoy informal conversations and meetings with coworkers. They also expect up-to-date technology.

Tell me to what you pay attention and I will tell you who you are.
JOSE ORTEGA Y GASSET

In 1924, researchers in the Western Electric Hawthorne plant near Chicago, Illinois, were attempting to determine the effect that lighting and working conditions had on productivity. The researchers adjusted the lighting in a variety of ways and measured the impact on output. Each time the lighting was adjusted, productivity increased. The employees' working conditions were also changed (i.e., hours, breaks), and productivity improved with each change. Interestingly, by the time the working conditions and lighting were returned to their original levels, absenteeism had plummeted and productivity was at its highest level.

When the researchers couldn't determine a pattern to the lighting or working conditions, they began to look elsewhere and realized that the productivity increase could be attributed to the attention the researchers were paying to the workers and not to the environmental effect at all. This discovery would greatly influence the social sciences in the decades that followed. The result is called the Hawthorne Effect or the Observer Effect. Individuals positively modify their behavior in response to being observed.

There are many things leaders can do to create an environment that allows people to work at their inventive and productive best. Perhaps the most important thing is also one of the simplest. Paying attention to someone doesn't require a financial investment. It's an energetic investment.

YOUR INVISIBLE TOOLBOX

When you pay attention to people, they respond.

Pay attention

77

A CANOPY OPEN TO NEW SUNLIGHT

According to Gallup, 87 percent of millennials rate professional or career growth and development opportunities as important to them in a job. This is an especially impressive number when compared with the 69 percent of non-millennials who say the same thing.

This deep interest in professional development may be the single most important differentiator for millennials in the workforce. The desire to learn and grow makes millennials well positioned to take advantage of the opportunities presented by the unprecedented changes that are expected to continue in the business environment.

Leadership and learning are indispensable to each other.
JOHN F. KENNEDY

Are you saddened when you see fallen trees after a strong storm? This change in the landscape, the result of natural causes, not only creates a sense of loss, it also opens up the possibility for a new landscape.

Scholar and futurist Joel Barker posed the following question: Which plant species is best positioned to take advantage of the prime real estate that comes available when a large tree falls and opens the canopy to new sunlight?

According to Barker, the common thinking was that the most competitive plant would prevail. Like many things, modern research has changed that thinking. It turns out that not the most competitive plants, but rather those in the best position to take advantage of the opportunity when it presents itself win the battle for the coveted niche.

Of course that makes sense. If the most competitive plant won every battle, then the entire forest would be populated by the same species. In nature, as in business, diversity is the spice of life. Small, sometimes extremely fragile plants are able to find a niche in which they don't just survive but thrive despite competitive pressures from all around. This is also true of many businesses.

This insight from the natural world is both excellent and concerning news. It provides great hope that the changes that are constant in the marketplace, if properly prepared for, may present great opportunities for the future. It also provides evidence that enjoying market leadership may be short-lived if preparation for the changes of the future doesn't remain at the forefront of a leader's strategic agenda.

How quickly do changes happen? In high-tech industries, they can happen multiple times in a single year. Although they experience change more slowly, in other markets such as the funeral industry, leaders are facing new challenges they've never seen at any time in the past that are reshaping business models. New technology introduces new possibilities to memorializing a loved one. Rising social interest in concerns about land use is leading people to make different choices around their final decisions.

Whether at the cellular level, the personal level, the organizational level, the national level, or the international level, everything is changing.

YOUR INVISIBLE TOOLBOX

Are you positioned to take advantage of opportunities presented when the landscape of your business environment changes?

Learn something new

78

IT'S ALL POSSIBLE

Millennials say they want purposeful lives. They are largely optimistic, believing that life and work should both have meaning. They are pushing for change on a large scale. They are challenging the providers of their products and services and the leaders of organizations and governments at an unprecedented rate.

Millennials are also self-reliant. They view societal, religious, and political organizations with a healthy skepticism. The solution for many of them is to fix things themselves. They approach challenges not just with technology as would be expected but also with new forms of social interaction. What inspirational stories will be told in the future about this generation?

If your actions inspire others to dream more, learn more, do more,
and become more, you are a leader.
JOHN QUINCY ADAMS

An example of self-reliance and meaningful impact is powerfully illustrated in the inspiring story of Terry Fox.

In 1977, eighteen-year-old Terry Fox lost his right leg to cancer. After such a tragedy, many people would give up. Fox wanted to make a difference. He had survived cancer but realized others might not. He wanted to raise $1 million for cancer research.

On April 12, 1980, twenty-one-year-old Fox began a journey he called the Marathon of Hope by dipping his artificial limb into the harbor at Saint John's, Newfoundland. His goal was to run a marathon a day across Canada and finish his journey by dipping his artificial limb into the seawater at Vancouver's Stanley Park near his home in Port Coquitlam, British Columbia. He trained hard for fifteen months, running a total of 3,159 miles. He frequently trained until his stump was raw and bleeding.

The money started to pour in as he gained publicity, and he expanded his goal to raise $24 million, one dollar for every Canadian. The support of people lining his route shouting "Don't give up, you can make it!" inspired him to continue.

On September 1, Terry ran his last mile near Thunder Bay, Ontario. Icy storms, blistering heat, and bitter winds hadn't deterred him. It was his medical condition that forced him to stop after running 3,339 miles.

At the hospital it was discovered that the cancer had spread to his lungs. Fox resolved to continue the fight. When his father was overheard to say it was unfair, Terry told him, "I don't feel this is unfair. That's the thing about cancer. I'm not the only one. It happens all the time to other people. I'm not special. This just intensifies what I did. It gives it more meaning. It'll inspire more people. I could have sat on my rear end, I could have forgotten what I'd seen in the hospital, but I didn't."

Terry Fox died from cancer on June 28, 1981. Flags throughout the nation were flown at half-mast. He had inspired and engaged others in his dream. He had made the difference he aspired to make. He met his fundraising goals, challenged people's attitudes toward the disabled, and showed everyone what unbreakable spirit is. His story didn't end with his death.

The first Terry Fox Run was held that September, and more than three hundred thousand people walked, ran, or cycled in his memory to raise money for cancer research. More than three decades later, Terry Fox Runs continue to take place in over nine thousand communities across Canada every year.

Among his many honors, Fox was the youngest to receive the Companion of the Order of Canada, the nation's top civilian honor. His portrait was hung in the Sports Hall of Fame. A mountain was named after him in British Columbia.

It's all possible if you're willing to dream and work hard enough to overcome challenges.

YOUR INVISIBLE TOOLBOX

Living up to aspirations of changing the world and making a difference will provide future generations with inspiration and many more stories like those of Terry Fox.

Dream and work hard

79

WHOSE LIFE IS IT ANYWAY?

It is more a matter of believing the good than of seeing it as
the fruit of our efforts.
CHUANG TZU

Legacies. We create daily what we will eventually leave. The real influence of our work more often than not is closely related to who we are and the times we live in.

It is not uncommon to find men and women who have left visible legacies that trace back to the roots of their youth. Ideals and situations from their childhood often show up later in their successes. Charles M. Schulz, the creator of the lovable and profitable Peanuts comic strip, is a good example. The world dearly loved and appreciated the bits and pieces of his life woven together in the form of his comic strip, which became a $20 million business. From Schulz's alter ego Charlie Brown we learned lessons, smiled, and saw our own lives differently due to his vision. We remember him for it.

Schulz's online biography states that from birth, comics played an important role in his life. At just two days old, an uncle nicknamed him Sparky after the horse Spark Plug from the Barney Google comic strip. Throughout his youth Schulz and his father shared a Sunday morning ritual of reading the funnies. Schulz was very proud when Ripley's newspaper feature "Believe It or Not" published his drawing of the family dog in 1937 at age fifteen.

Charles Schulz fell madly in love in his teens with a redheaded girl who influenced the characters of Lucy and Peppermint Patty in his cartoon strip. His experiences in life were not always happy (his declared first love married another man, a loss that haunted Schulz all his life) but these experiences, reflected in the character interactions of the strip, became the brick and mortar of his business and his legacy.

Legacies often greatly illustrate the times we live in. Richard Graham is remembered most for his efforts in 1965 to abolish gender-based employment advertisements. "Help Wanted Male" and "Help Wanted Female" ads were no longer legal by 1968 in the United States due to his efforts. Graham went on to manage the Center for Moral Education at Harvard, founded the Goddard–Cambridge Center for Social Change at Goddard College, and served as an advisor to the Washington-based Council for Research in Values and Psychology, among many other accomplishments. Yet what he did for gender equity specifically colored and was colored by the times he lived in.

Alongside Graham's legacy is that of Natalie Gleboff, director of the School of American Ballet in New York. Hired by George Balanchine in the 1940s, her Russian background (she was born in Romania) and experience living and adapting in the United States (she came to New York with her UN interpreter husband after World War Two) created her legacy. Gleboff is remembered for bringing a "perfect blend of dynastic order and new world energy" to carry out Balanchine's principles while directing the growth of the ballet company from the 1940s to the 1970s. The ballerinas of the school remembered her as "tempering her Russian authority with wisdom and kindness." In the social climate of the times, she brought to her work knowledge and expertise of Russia, ballet, Balanchine, and adaptation to the United States that few others could have had in those years. The times we live in do help determine the legacy we leave to the world.

When then does one's legacy really begin? Recognizing the influence of your life experiences and the necessities of the times you're living in places you on the path of a legacy only you can leave. You have everything you need within and around you to shape and paint what your legacy might be. Visible and noted by the world or not, your legacy will be uniquely your own. What you will be remembered for is something the world and those around you are in need of and are waiting for, right now.

YOUR INVISIBLE TOOLBOX

Look at yourself, your life, your work, and reflect on them.
What aspects of your present day legacy are rooted in your early experiences and/or the times you are living in?

Begin living your legacy

Part V

TOOLS FOR PERSONAL GROWTH

We are all engaged in two battles.

In the internal world there is an endless contest between the two sides of self. It is the conflict between our light side and our dark side.

Then there is the external world where we must relate to others. A struggle wages as we figure out how to best interact with the people we like and to coexist with those we don't. Daily, we must navigate relationships with those we agree with and those we oppose. We wrestle with how to best harmonize with those who are friends and deal with those who are foes.

Despite the advances that have resulted from technological innovations, the fact remains that businesses are still about people. Effectiveness, therefore, requires effective people skills. The best place to start understanding people is to understand ourselves, our strengths and blemishes. Only then can we begin to understand others and choose actions and reactions suited to the wide range of interpersonal situations we encounter.

In this part of the book, we examine the tools for self-discovery and personal growth.

Once we believe in ourselves, we can risk curiosity, wonder, spontaneous delight, or any experience that reveals the human spirit.
E. E. CUMMINGS

80

SEND IN THE CLOWNS

Not too long ago, clown sightings dominated the news. Scary clowns popped up in almost every region of the United States, prompting a frenzy of fear and even making their way into the White House in official daily briefings. The hysteria prompted even the likes of Stephen King to tweet out a call to chill about the matter and recognize clowns for what they are supposed to be: cheerful caricatures to make us laugh. Yet the scary ones do not match that supposition.

So what does this fear phenomenon tell us about fear itself? What does it tell us about us? Charles Dickens, the renowned English writer, identified what we really fear in the image of a clown. "What fascinates us is not the exaggerated painted face, or the dull face of a man underneath. It's the tension between the two. The dissonance between what is and what appears to be."

In the interpersonal aspect of our professional lives we may often feel dissonance between "what is and what appears to be," as Dickens cited, that turns into fear. The dissonance between how we see ourselves (or how we are self-promoted by others) and how others might see us when we are asked to interpersonally interact in ways we do not feel competent creates tension. This tension and the resulting dissonance can create real fear.

What interpersonal situations at work create dissonance? Anything that stretches your interpersonal abilities and/or comfort level. Here are a few examples:

    • When asked to manage someone who was formerly a peer, you don't see how that person will see you as a leader when you were once his or her colleague.

    • When you're leading a change that you don't fully believe is in the best interest of your department yet you must promote it.

    • When you're asked to give a board presentation and know your presentation style doesn't reflect your true ability.

- Although very competent in your job, when asked to entertain a client, you know you'll struggle with small talk and informal interactions.
- Your social media presence doesn't communicate your desired professional presence.

Many interpersonal interactions at work are feared due to the dissonance they cause. The possibility of feeling exposed, that you won't measure up with the expectations someone has of you due to the job or role you hold when asked to interact interpersonally. A disconnect between how you appear in one context and how you're perceived in another. The potential fears wrapped up in interpersonal interactions are endless, but you don't have to let these fears escalate and run amok with your career.

> *Nothing in life is to be feared. It is only to be understood.*
> MARIE CURIE

Luckily the interpersonal fears you may hold professionally are far easier to address and dispel than the dissonance and fear the creepy clown sightings elicit in the general population.

The only way to combat fear is to identify it accurately and get specific support. Identification requires asking yourself, "What is creating this feeling of dissonance for me?" Once this is identified, you can address the issue and find support.

YOUR INVISIBLE TOOLBOX

In terms of the interpersonal nature of your professional life, support comes in the form of skills. Interpersonal skills are readily available to you and are best learned by you alone.

Identify your fears

81

STRESSED OUT

According to the American Psychological Association, millennials experience more stress and are less able to manage it than any other generation. They're also more anxious than older Americans. Twelve percent of millennials are said to have a diagnosed anxiety disorder—almost twice the percentage of boomers.

Does this mean all others manage stress more effectively? Is responding with anxiety unique to millennials?

Stress is inherent even in the animal kingdom. Visualize a cat in hot pursuit of a mouse. The cat catches the mouse. Good day for the cat, bad day for the mouse.

Or what if the mouse outmaneuvers the cat? Bad day for the cat. Good day for the mouse.

Similar to cats and mice, humans are hardwired for a fight or flight response when faced with a stressful situation. Where the cat is competing to acquire a meal and the mouse is fleeing the threat of becoming a meal, humans have different stressors.

If our automatic stress response perceives the threat cannot be outrun (flight) or outfought (fight), we freeze. Imagine a deer in the headlights or the paralyzed possum "playing dead."

Our three-fold automatic stress response is simply this:

- Fight
- Flee
- Freeze

The response is quick and efficient. When challenged, it sorts through the millions of sensory bits of data we are exposed to. Like a filter, it screens the information for level of importance and tells us whether to react or not.

The amygdala in the emotional center sees and hears everything that occurs
to us instantaneously and is the trigger point for the fight or flight response.
DANIEL GOLEMAN

Every bit of sensory stimuli we perceive is screened for two qualities.

· Is this information of value?

· Is this information of threat?

If the answer is no to both questions, the data is screened out. Gone. If yes, we are going to fight, flight, or freeze.

Is the leaf falling to the ground behind you important? No, so data is screened out.

Is the oncoming car important? Well, if you happen to be in the path of it, the answer is clearly yes, and the filter springs into action to alert you to the danger.

Instinct does not send critical information to higher thinking centers to be contemplated by committee in pursuit of a decision. Instead, instinct forwards the alert to a different frontier, the physiological response center. The information bypasses the higher brain centers and ignites your physiology to respond. Your heart rate increases, your large muscle groups prepare, all in a split second, and the fight or flight response (in the case of the oncoming vehicle, the response is flight) responds to the call.

You move—without any creative thought.

If you don't rely on your instinct and instead pause to contemplate the context of the situation thoroughly, you may find yourself facing a tragic end.

Instinct is a useful and automatic survival response. It resides in the unconscious. It is especially useful when facing a physical threat. You don't have to think about responding. You just will.

The fight or flight response also engages when the threat is a psychological one. Psychological threats in the workplace and life are prevalent.

Think of a time when a customer, manager, friend, relative, or team member overtly disagreed with you. Even though words and a disagreement cannot physically hurt you, your physiology responds. On the physiological level, the response activates regardless of whether you're facing the threat of your work being challenged or the threat of an approaching stranger wielding a weapon.

This causes you to resort to unproductive methods of interacting and often unintended results.

- In behavioral terms when the reaction is a psychological one, the flight response manifests as passive, accommodating or avoiding behaviors like shutting down or giving in.
- The fight response expresses as aggressive, competitive, or attacking behavior like yelling or demanding.
- In the workplace or in life, the freeze response is experienced as "going blank" when challenged, as in a meeting. Although you might cognitively have something to say, you're stopped in your tracks and can't engage.

Classic interpersonal responses in situations involving differences with others are hard or soft. This happens for all humans, not just millennials. Hard is the fight response and a win-at-all costs approach. Soft is the flight response where an individual attempting to avoid tension makes too many concessions or gives in.

Every profession and life situation presents challenges in its own way. When challenged, humans are put on the spot and need to respond. Many people go with their natural instincts and get passive or aggressive. Yet they don't need to become defensive or attack. They can choose other behaviors.

YOUR INVISIBLE TOOLBOX

When someone is skilled at choosing versus reacting, you may not even notice. You just see the impact and may attribute it to qualities such as leadership, charisma, or intelligence.

Identify your stressors

—————— 82 ——————

TOP FLOOR THINKING

What lies behind us and what lies before us are small matters
when compared to what lies within us.
RALPH WALDO EMERSON

Millennials have witnessed multiple major events that have shaped not only how they view the world but what causes them concern. 9/11, world terrorism, the recession, and many more critical events threaten basic survival. How does the capacity to think clearly help people process and experience these events?

One of the key differences between human beings and animals is the higher thinking centers humans possess. Cognitive thought, creativity, and innovation were secondary needs to our early ancestors. In the past, avoiding becoming a dinner entrée for the saber-toothed tiger around the next bend was of great importance. As daily physical threats became less severe, humans expanded into spending more time using the higher parts of their brains.

Important inventions like the wheel happened only because certain individuals managed to survive the threats of the day. This left them free to exercise their creative abilities and tackle problems that impacted civilization. A clear privilege of being human is the ability to positively impact life rather than simply react to life's untenable situations.

What do the crew of US Airways flight 1549, firefighters, and the Diavolo Dance Troupe have in common? Before we speculate, let's explore each individually.

- US Airways flight 1549: After hitting a flock of Canada geese upon takeoff, both engines of the Airbus A320 were disabled. The captain and his crew determined they needed to land the plane on the Hudson River. Amazingly, all 155 crew members and passengers survived the crash landing.

• Firefighters: These brave men and women are willing to make the ultimate sacrifice to save people they've never met. They routinely respond to a wide variety of emergency situations, from saving someone from a burning building to protecting animals, property, and the environment from a range of threats.

• Diavolo Dance Troupe: Founded by Jacques Heim in 1992, all performances of this troupe are done by dancers using oversized man-made wooden structures. The dancers describe their work as "architecture in motion." Their performances blend acrobatics and modern dance in a physically grueling presentation.

So what do these three groups have in common?

You may be thinking one or all of the following:

• Risk

• Trust

• Danger

• Teamwork

If so, you're right. All of those are true. Yet there is one other characteristic that these groups share, a most challenging one, especially in times of stress like landing a plane in unfamiliar conditions, saving someone from a burning building, or dancing with a large-scale moving structure.

US Airways flight 1549

When the media interviewed the pilot of flight 1549, Captain Chesley "Sully" Sullenberger, about the water landing, he was asked whether or not he was praying during the crisis. He calmly responded no and added that he imagined those in the back of the plane had that covered. "I was doing what I was trained to do," explained the captain. This was an action that required him to override his natural instincts.

Firefighters

Our natural instinctual programming causes us to run away from burning buildings. Highly trained firefighters run into a burning building. They dedicate their entire career to learning the nuances of each individual type of fire and other dangerous situations they may encounter so that when required they can handle the situation expertly, safely, and with the best outcome possible. They override the instinct to flee.

Diavolo Dance Troupe

In an interview before a performance, one of the Diavolo dancers was asked about the hardest challenge in being part of the dance team. She responded that one might think it's maintaining the necessary level of physical fitness required, but it isn't. Nor is it mastering the complex choreography. When the oversized structures in the Diavolo dances move, the dancers perform by falling into them. The toughest thing, the dancer affirmed, is "overcoming the body's natural tendency to resist the fall."

Along with trust, teamwork, risk, and danger, a common element of these three disparate groups is the ability to access higher-level thinking in times of stress and challenge.

You may have used this higher thinking if you were in New York on 9/11, or when you found the job market impenetrable in 2009. It isn't easy to override natural impulses, but doing so can be learned and realized. The ability to accomplish this is an important force field to possess.

YOUR INVISIBLE TOOLBOX

As a human being, you have free will. You don't have to behave according to the natural fight, flight, or freeze response. You can train yourself to overcome your natural programming and employ your higher thinking centers to choose the most appropriate behaviors for the situation.

Choose your behavior

83

LESSONS FROM THE PLAYGROUND

According to Ernst & Young's Global Generation Research, nearly one-third of millennials say that balancing work, family, and personal life has become more difficult in the past five years. Forty-seven percent are working more hours. This compares with 38 percent of generation X and only 28 percent of baby boomers.

Do you remember going to a playground to ride a teeter-totter as a child? Or have you taken your own children to play on one? If so, you've learned something about balance.

A teeter-totter is a large rectangle that is balanced in the middle on a central sphere. One person hops on one end and one on the other. You take turns being elevated in the air while your friend touches the ground, pushes off, and vice versa. Every now and then your friend might not balance well, or push off incorrectly, or prematurely exit his or her end to leave you crashing abruptly down to earth. From this you kinesthetically learn that balance takes paying attention and a bit of trust.

For children, there is not much to balance in life short of the teeter-totter. As we grow into working adults, raising families, contributing to our communities, and trying to continue to evolve as people, finding balance can seem as jolting as the crashing to the ground of the teeter-totter.

Research shows that 61 percent of us worry about our work–life balance, 70 percent of us have had our health affected by it, 59 percent of us feel it affects our interpersonal relationships in the form of stress, and it is a leading cause of workplace violence and absenteeism. It often feels as if we have more to do than the time to do it in. Attempting to attend to diverse responsibilities can leave us feeling effective in none of them.

How do we balance work and life in a way that everything receives its due and we feel successful in all our roles?

We may be able to take some tips from athletes.

Gymnast Shawn Johnson exemplified the utmost professionalism and athletic prowess in her events at the Olympics games. Watching her get ready to compete on the balance beam was telling. After Johnson powdered up her hands, the camera focused in on a clear shot of her face. It was impossible not to see the combination of focus and determination there. It was evident that although she was in an arena with thousands of people, she was clearly not in that noisy, stressful space at all. Her look communicated there were only two things at that moment she was present with, the balance beam and herself.

Olympic swimmer Michael Phelps also gave us a glimpse of this same presence while stealing the show in all his events. At one of them, newscasters were speculating whether he would win and if he was getting stressed. The newscaster said, "Watch his face as he comes up for air. If his face shows any tension, it's over. His body will tense and he will not win." Although the race was close, as Phelps's head bobbed up for a breath before his turn, he looked calm. He is too savvy of a swimmer not to have known his challenges at that moment, but he did not let the challenge register in his body and affect his result.

What do the actions of these two Olympians tell us about balance? About work–life balance? Too often people picture success as balancing work and life perfectly at all times—always the right amount of time and equal time for family, work, community, etc. Like a teeter-totter that stays constant in a parallel position. This is not only impossible but impractical. Perfect balance is not desirable. There are times in life when we need to devote more to one aspect of our existence than another.

There's no such thing as work–life balance. There are work–life choices, and you make them, and they have consequences.
JACK WELCH

So what is desirable work–life balance? What does it look like? Like the athlete, we have true work–life balance when we achieve a natural fluidity in moving from one necessary context of our lives to the next and being fully present in each. So if we're at home, we're not thinking about the details of our workday or the pressures around it. Instead we focus like Shawn Johnson on the task or person right in front of us, and we are fully present. We give it our all in that space of time.

Conversely, if we're at work, we powder up, create the space for our task and expertise to combine and execute. If there are home issues, we check them at the door. We're more effective in the work moment, which will get us back to the home context quicker and after having achieved more. Like Michael Phelps, our body language never reflects tension or stress over an outcome. Instead, it remains indicative of our calm focus and intent to do our best in that moment.

YOUR INVISIBLE TOOLBOX

Like most things in life, work–life balance sounds easier than it is. It's a discipline, an agreement you make with yourself, and it can be achieved. The one thing that will not change is the fact that paying attention to what's in front of you and within you at any given time, fully present in the moment, will allow you to create a work–life balance that is definitely medal worthy.

Be fully present

—————————— 84 ——————————

THE MYTH OF MULTITASKING

Of all the beliefs people hold about millennials, the one that is touted as a great strength is their ability to multitask. Employers seem to covet this ability. After all, doing two things at once must be better than doing one thing at a time, right? It seems so intuitively simple and logical.

One of the most enduring myths around personal efficiency and time management is that multitasking saves time. Evidence of the widespread belief in this myth comes from the more than six million web pages offering strategies about how to multitask.

But the research on the subject of multitasking does not support this myth. In fact, quite the opposite is true. Multitasking actually slows people down and leads to errors and increased stress.

In his book *The One Thing*, Gary Keller sites a 2009 study conducted by Clifford Nass, a professor at Stanford University, designed to determine what made for a great multitasker. There were 262 test subjects in his study, divided into two groups. One group was made up of high multitaskers. The other was low multitaskers. The assumption was that the multitaskers would outperform the other group.

Nass was wrong. It turned out that the high multitaskers were outperformed on every measure. While they were all convinced that they were great at doing two things at once, the research clearly showed they were lousy at it.

When you try to do two things at once, you either can't do it or you won't do either task as well. It is a recipe for losing efficiency and effectiveness.

Why?

Your brain is hardwired to focus. Focus on one thing at a time.

If you chase two rabbits, both will escape.
ANCIENT PROVERB

Does trying to read the news updates crawling across the bottom of the television screen while attending to the main program frustrate you? Do you get engaged in the interview and then catch a glimpse of the end of a news update "...dead at twenty-one"? Do you spend the next twenty minutes trying to figure out who died?

Can't you walk and chew gum at the same time? Yes, but that's because there's no channel interference going on in your brain. Two different parts of the brain are used for those two activities. Walking and carrying on a conversation is a breeze on familiar terrain. If you were walking over treacherous terrain, the casual conversation would stop so you could concentrate on walking. Similarly, you can drive your car while listening to music or audio books. Until you find yourself driving in a blinding storm, and then the noise is a distraction because the unconscious activity of driving has necessarily become conscious because of the danger. You must focus.

Can we do two things at once? On the condition that one of the two things is habitual and unconsciously done (not requiring creative or cognitive thought).

Many of the things we try to do at the same time use the same part of the brain. For example, the activities of e-mailing and talking on the phone both use the communication center. When we try to do both activities at the same time, we miss something. When we try to read the scrolling updates at the bottom of the television screen while also listening to the media interview, our attempts at multitasking fail and we miss something. When we're working on an expense report and a colleague drops by to talk about a business problem, the relative complexity of those two tasks makes it difficult to jump back and forth. This takes a toll on productivity.

What do multitasking and interruptions cost? It depends on the complexity of the tasks. Researcher Dr. David Meyer reports that the time lost can range from 25 percent on simple tasks to more than 100 percent on complex tasks.

Multitasking also takes a toll on relationships. When we attempt to listen to a loved one at home while also checking our device for messages, the other party realizes that he or he doesn't have our full attention, and the cost goes beyond lost efficiency—relationships also suffer.

All of us can quickly enjoy improvements in productivity, decreases in errors, and reductions in stress by applying this insight to our lives.

YOUR INVISIBLE TOOLBOX

When two activities demand your complete attention, choose one. The next time you find yourself reading an e-mail while talking on the phone, texting while driving, checking your device in a meeting, completing a puzzle while interacting with your kids, reading PowerPoint slides while listening to a speaker, pause and remind yourself to focus on one task at a time.

Focus

85

$86,400 EACH AND EVERY DAY

A typical millennial is faced with what seems to be a never-ending day. Millennials grew up with heavier schedules than the generations that preceded them, shuttling between some or all of the following: school, athletic practice, religious study, tutoring sessions, volunteer activities, part-time jobs, friends, and family. There's little time to do much else but sleep, eat, and repeat the routine the next day. These constant activities may have led to wonderful growth opportunities. They may also have led to time management stress as millennials quickly learned to overschedule themselves. Does this pattern describe you?

You've probably learned by now that life isn't the same for everyone. While all of us have resources, there is great disparity between those who have many and those who have few. Some have more money than others while others have more energy, creativity, or technical ability than the next.

However, there is one great equalizer. It is time. No matter how talented, energetic, rich or poor, each of us has an equal amount of hours per day. The ways we choose to spend our time is a reflection not only of our biological needs but also our values. Amid clamoring demands, we can vote for that which we feel is most important. We vote with our time.

What would you do if you were given the gift of $86,400 each and every morning, but if you didn't spend or invest the money it would disappear at the end of the day, never to be returned? In other words, it cannot be accumulated.

Each and every person is given a gift just like the $86,400 each and every day. It's the gift of 86,400 seconds. We can spend it or invest it anyway we like, but at the end of the day it's gone. We all have the same amount of time. It's how we invest it that determines how closely we come to reaching our goals.

Efforts and courage are not enough without purpose and direction.
JOHN F. KENNEDY

Most of us spend our days putting out fires, allowing little time to proactively attend to issues not yet at crisis stage. We seek relief by spending hours in time-wasting activities that may feel relaxing in the moment and frustrate us later when we perceive we've wasted them.

Should our main goal in life be getting as much as possible done? Or should it be getting the most important things done? What are the most important things?

YOUR INVISIBLE TOOLBOX

What are your goals? Devote part of every day to activities that answer the question, "What one thing could I be doing that will move me closer to achieving one of my goals?"

Set goals

---------- 86 ----------

IT COSTS NOTHING, UNLESS IT WORKS

Millennials are said to have new ideas for where, how, and when work should take place. The nine-to-five traditional workdays of the past are being discarded in favor of more flexible and mobile work schedules that leverage technological resources. While it's easy to argue for the merits of these work options, there's a dark side to being constantly connected. Not surprisingly, millennials who also express an interest in balance and quality of life wrestle with a paradox. How can "always connected to work" and "quality of life" coexist? Always "on," many millennials struggle with the very work environments they say they crave.

In the eighteenth century, economist Vilfredo Pareto developed what is popularly known as the 80/20 Rule, or the Pareto Principle. This rule states that 80 percent of the value of a group of activities is generally concentrated in only 20 percent of those activities.

Stated differently, nearly four-fifths of our efforts are wasted.

Concentrate on the essentials... we will then be accomplishing
the greatest results with the effort expended.
TED W. ENGSTROM AND R. ALEC MACKENZIE

Although many activities are carried out every day, the critical few are the ones to target in improving your personal effectiveness. What are the critical few?

In 1918, Ivy Lee, a renowned efficiency expert, was approached by Charles Schwab, who at the time was president of Bethlehem Steel. Schwab sought out Lee in hopes of finding better ways of getting things done. Lee is reported to have said, "I can increase your people's efficiency if you will allow me to spend just fifteen minutes with each of your executives."

"How much will it cost me?" the wealthy and astute industrialist asked.

Lee responded, "Nothing, unless it works. After three months, you can send me a check for whatever you feel it is worth."

The following day, Lee met for fifteen minutes with each of Schwab's top executives. He requested each one to commit to a specific practice for ninety days. He instructed them, before leaving the office at the end of the day, to make a list of the six most important things they had to do the next day. He then asked each executive to prioritize the items on the list in order of importance. Finally, he directed them to tackle the activities in order the next day and cross off each item after finishing it. Only then should they move on to the next item on the list. If something didn't get done, he told them, put it on the following day's list.

Each Bethlehem Steel executive consented to follow Lee's instructions. Three months later, Schwab studied the results and was so pleased that he sent Lee a check for $25,000. In an era when the average American worker was paid 56 cents per hour, this was a huge sum.

YOUR INVISIBLE TOOLBOX

If Schwab, one of the smartest businessmen of his day, was willing to pay so much money for this advice, maybe you should consider trying it out. A century and many technological advances later, this timeless prioritization practice still delivers impressive results.

Prioritize your activities

87

THERE IS ALWAYS MORE TO THE STORY

It is commonly believed that millennials hook up for the purposes of sex more frequently than preceding generations. This perception may come from the growing number of dating apps available and the large number of social media posts by millennials chronicling their sexual exploits.

The facts tell a very different story. Things are not always as they appear to be. Gen Xers born in the late 1960s were more than twice as likely to have been sexually active as millennials born in the 1990s. Millennials who are sexually active have fewer partners than both Xers and boomers. The only generation comparable to millennials was born in the 1920s.

When presented with only part of the story, why do we jump to conclusions? Why do we assume facts that are not in evidence? Why don't we engage in conversations to learn more?

Rarely do we have the entire story. We form our impressions and judgments of situations most often with incomplete information. To do this we rely on shortcuts. We take in the sensory data available, look for patterns, interpret what we see, and add missing information for what we don't. When faced with conflicting data and the inevitable incomplete story, we trust mostly what we see. Consider the following true story.

A single mother was devoted to her only child, David. One day when David was a baby, his mother left him sleeping to go out and work in the garden. While she was in the garden, the house caught fire. Unconcerned with her own life and safety, she ran inside to save her son while witnesses to the event tried to hold her back.

Amazingly, she found David untouched and rescued him. During the rescue, her hair caught fire and burned her face, leaving horrific permanent scars.

Despite growing up to become successful, David was always embarrassed by his mother's appearance and would occasionally comment to others on her ugliness. When his mother heard this, she was saddened. She decided to confront him and tell him where the scars had come from.

She was killed in a bus crash on her way to see David to tell him the truth.

When searching through his mother's belongings, he found her journal. It included the following entries:

- September 5, 1980. I won the Miss Toronto Beauty Contest.
- January 14, 1982. My husband, Tonny Gateson, passed away in a road accident while I was six months pregnant.
- July 2, 1983. My face was scarred and I lost my hair saving my son, David, from a house fire.

There's always another story. There's more than meets the eye.
W. H. AUDEN

Should David be blamed for forming the impressions he held? Because he was short of complete information, he did what we all do. He pieced together the rest of the story and made a judgment. A decision he no doubt regrets.

YOUR INVISIBLE TOOLBOX

The tendency to jump to premature conclusions is part of human nature. When you remind yourself of this natural inclination, you can make different behavioral choices. Seek out the whole story and make a more informed decision.

Get the facts

88

SWEAT THE SMALL STUFF

It's been said that millennials haven't mastered the art of decision-making nor do they excel at attention to detail or time management. Whether this is a product of a maturing contingent of workers who will acquire these skills with experience or if it's a characteristic of the millennial cohort is unknown. What's important is addressing the deficiency before it limits career success.

It's the little details that are vital. Little things make big things happen.
JOHN WOODEN

Walter Pavlo earned a master's degree in finance from Mercer University in Macon, Georgia, and was a discontented senior manager at MCI Communications when he started taking advantage of the company's lax accounting standards. The small decisions he made over the course of time and a path of dishonesty and fraud resulted in a $6 million crime and two years in prison.

Post-prison, Pavlo now works with organizations and business schools to help others avoid the path he traveled. He makes the following point:

"It starts with a small decision that incrementally got worse and worse. You tell yourself your intentions are good at first, but then you find yourself in a place you don't recognize…it's tough to get back."

The path to corruption starts with a single step—usually a small one where it seems no one will get hurt and there are no consequences. Actions have outcomes. Behaviors have consequences. We can see how a series of small bad decisions and behaviors add up to enormous negative consequences.

So it is with small good decisions. While small behaviors and actions may not seem to have a meaningful impact or consequences, they do. This truth is hard for us to remember when we're inclined to believe that the big win comes from the big action. But small behaviors carried out consistently over time represent competitive advantage for modern organizations.

The Snowball: Warren Buffett and the Business of Life is a biography written by Wall Street analyst Alice Schroeder on the world's most famous investor. "Snowball" is a metaphor for describing the law of compound returns—the core investment concept for how wealth grows over time. A small snowball rolling downhill gathers mass, which increases speed, which continues to increase mass. The longer the hill, the larger the snowball grows. In investment terms, the longer the runway before retirement, the greater the opportunity to benefit from the law of compound returns.

The same law applies to human interactions. Over time, actions and behaviors consistently carried out multiply and ultimately become our brand. If they are positive human interactions, the brand is a positive one. If they are negative, so goes the brand.

Don't Sweat the Small Stuff... and it's all Small Stuff is one of the *Don't Sweat* series of best-selling books by Richard Carlson, Ph.D. Carlson, a recognized expert on stress reduction and happiness, inspires people to keep from getting bogged down with little things in life. The ability to manage stress, calm down, and achieve balance is a goal worth attaining. The sentiment of not sweating the small stuff, intended to preserve physical and emotional health, has a dark side.

Minimizing or rationalizing the effect of small things is a recipe for disaster, as Walter Pavlo learned when his small, dishonest actions added up to a serious crime and prison sentence. Similarly, minimizing the impact of small positive things can lead individuals and organizations to miss important opportunities.

If you take the time to understand and execute the small behaviors that lead to the positive outcomes, you will make more than money. You will be building an advantage that is difficult for competitors to copy.

Things don't have to change the world to be important.
STEVE JOBS

Taking pains with the wording in an e-mail to a client matters. Pausing to reconsider before texting a potentially offensive joke matters. Struggling with the best way to express your gratitude to a colleague matters. Wrestling with the various ways your message may be received by your boss matters. Rehearsing how you are going to talk to your child about values matters. It's all seemingly small stuff, but it matters.

While they may not seem like they matter in the moment, it's the accumulation of many small things over time that will shape your successes and failures and, ultimately, your character.

YOUR INVISIBLE TOOLBOX

Carefully considering each small decision you make may appear to slow progress in the short term, but it delivers impressive results in the long term.

Get small things right

89

SUCCESS WITHOUT FORCE

Millennials have been saddled with the label of impatience and described as the instant gratification generation. They are perceived as wanting to impact business results instantly. They expect to influence a customer experience immediately. They are believed to have disproportionate goals for their own career advancement and unrealistic expectations about the growth of their financial investments.

Is impatience a character flaw or a virtue? Is moving fast and expecting quick results a weakness or a strength?

In 1981, Pat Parelli founded Natural Horsemanship – The Parelli Program, a relationship-based approach to training human and horse. Parelli asserts that his prescribed method helps horse lovers achieve:

- Success without force
- Partnership without dominance
- Teamwork without fear
- Willingness without intimidation
- Harmony without coercion

When Pat Parelli says, "Take the time it takes so it takes less time," he is referring to the ground work and relationship building with the horse. "You take care of the small things first. Even though it feels like it takes a long time in the beginning, you don't create new problems and you ultimately end up with a better relationship with the animal."

Parelli has earned worldwide recognition for the success of his approach. The method works with horses. It also works with people. It is a formula for success in all relationships. When we take the time it takes, it takes less time.

"Taking extra time" are certainly unpopular words in our fast-paced world of multitasking, instant solutions, and McEverything. Nevertheless, some things take time. Sometimes we need to pause and remind ourselves of this.

The popular business press advocates the importance of maximizing strengths of people and that, for the most part, overcoming weaknesses is a waste of precious time. That it takes far more time and energy to move from incompetence to mediocrity than to move from competence to excellence.

Many people, especially those with great strengths in specific areas, adapt this insight into an excuse for not knowing anything (or knowing very little) about other areas. This is intellectual arrogance and is quite different than having no strength.

> *Ninety-nine percent of the failures come from people who*
> *have the habit of making excuses.*
> GEORGE WASHINGTON CARVER

Consider highly technically skilled individuals like engineers, accountants, scientists, and technicians who report, "I am not a people person" and defiantly oppose any situation that requires them to work effectively with people unlike themselves. Similarly, professionals in areas like marketing, sales, and human resources often pride themselves on their ignorance of basic processes or elementary accounting.

Although our goal should always be to build on our strengths, can't almost everyone acquire enough skill or knowledge not to be completely incompetent about it?

YOUR INVISIBLE TOOLBOX

No one can escape the fact that defects and weaknesses matter. Success depends not only on moving steadily forward but on preventing derailment. Preventing derailment means going beyond nourishing strengths and attending to flaws. That type of development takes time.

Take the time it takes

—————————————— 90 ——————————————

PRACTICE MAKES PERMANENT

Millennials are believed to learn differently from the generations that preceded them. Short attention spans lead to a preference for bite-sized information and an interest in quick and easy access to just-in-time resources. What does this mean for your own growth and development?

Have you ever tried to improve your golf game? Have hours on the driving range, money, and time spent with the golf pro and dozens of rounds on the golf course resulted in mastery of the game?

Most of us are convinced that if we simply practice enough, our game will improve. But countless hours of practice on the course and payments for lessons often lead to unremarkable results.

What's missing? Is even more time required?

Maestro, mentor, and polio survivor Itzhak Perlman had the following wisdom to share on the subject of practice.

"As a child, I hated to practice. But practicing is an art; it's not just about putting in the time. A lot of kids are too young to immediately get that. They say, well, I'm going to do my four or five hours a day, and I'm going to keep repeating everything and it's going to be good. And sometimes they wonder why it's not working. You need to organize practice; you need a goal. You need to ask yourself, 'Why am I practicing and what is it for?' Sometimes the repetition without thinking can be counterproductive. If you practice something wrong—without knowing it—then you have to undo it by practicing even more. If you practice slowly and with a brain, you will save a lot of time. You can accomplish in an hour what could take a week."

Does practice make perfect? It's more accurate to say that practice makes permanent. This is an insight embraced by the masters across a wide range of fields, including interpersonal skills.

YOUR INVISIBLE TOOLBOX

The key to perfection is acquiring skills, setting specific goals, and practice. Only that, not mindlessly repeating the way things have always been done, is the intelligent approach to mastery.

Practice mindfully

91

IN THE ZONE

More than a third of millennials say they are superstitious, but that number may decline in the years ahead as they age. Surveys reveal that younger people tend to be more superstitious than older people.

A black cat crossing your path signifies that the animal is going somewhere.
GROUCHO MARX

Where do superstitions come from? Is there any validity to them? Before you skip this chapter thinking it's all a bunch of baloney, consider these stories from the world of sports.

The rumors and stories are true that Jason Giambi, a famous baseball player, wore a golden thong to bring him out of batting slumps. He received the thong as a joke, but he claimed that it helped him and, later, other players as well. Derek Jeter was in a slump of 0-for-32. After putting on the thong, he hit a homer on the first pitch. Although that was the only time Jeter wore the thong, he still believes in its magic, as do other players.

Giambi hung the thong in players' lockers whenever he believed they needed luck. Catcher Jorge Posada said, "Whoever is on slumps puts it on. A lot of players have worn it." Although no one can really say how the thong works, Giambi says it has always worked for the players.

Giambi isn't the only famous athlete to try for a competitive advantage by tapping the mysterious powers of a lucky item that will get him into the zone.

- Consider entire teams who change their eating habits, alter their hygiene routines, or refuse to shave during playoffs for fear it will negatively sway momentum.
- Tiger Woods famously wears red shirts in the final round of a tournament. Whether it's because his mom told him to or honoring

his alma mater, Stanford, or trying to instill fear in his opponents with the power color is unknown. But he's clearly employing an intentional pattern that's designed to give him an edge.

• Michael Jordan achieved sports world immortality due in part to his beloved college shorts that he wore under his uniform.

• The great one, Wayne Gretzky, claimed a touch of baby powder on his hockey stick contributed to his greatness.

Articles of clothing, symbolic items, treasured photographs, favorite scents, certain music, routines, prayers are all examples of triggers people tap to get them into the zone for peak performance.

Does the thong, baby powder, altered hygiene, or red shirt actually shape the outcome of a game? What is more likely is that the lucky item laser focuses the attention of the performer on the goal. Setting a goal, setting sincere attention behind it, and choosing a physical symbol to constantly remind you of your goal are all excellent strategies for continuously keeping your focus and triggering your attention on the achievement of your goals.

YOUR INVISIBLE TOOLBOX

The use of a trigger and the results are not limited to the world of athletics.

Select a trigger

92

MORE THAN LUCK

Millennials are the most educated generation in history. Unfortunately, the college degree deemed essential to career success is no longer unlocking doors as advertised. Millennials have higher levels of student loan debt, poverty, and unemployment than prior generations. They also have lower levels of wealth and personal income than previous generations at this stage in their lives. Not unexpectedly, they report higher levels of clinical anxiety, stress, and depression than any other generation at the same age.

How can they overcome these daunting obstacles? Is there a way to see a bright future beyond the overwhelming fog that hangs over the present?

Consider these inspiring true stories.

American swimmer Florence Chadwick was the first woman ever to cross the English Channel twice both ways. At thirty-four, she was determined to be the first woman to swim the Catalina Channel to the coast of California. The event attracted a large television audience.

As it so often is, the California coast was blanketed in fog that fourth of July morning in 1952. Chadwick was undaunted, although the environment was hostile. She fought the bone-chilling cold waters, and several times sharks had to be driven away with rifles. Pushed to her limits, she started to doubt her ability to complete the task. Fifteen hours and fifty-five minutes into the swim, she asked her trainer and her mother, who were in one of the boats accompanying her, to take her out of the water. They urged her to continue, but she insisted she couldn't and was pulled into the boat.

Chadwick was devastated when she discovered she was only a half mile from the California coast. "Look, I'm not excusing myself," she told a reporter, "but if I could have seen land, I know I could have made it." The cold water and the sharks didn't defeat her. It was the fog. She couldn't see her goal.

Two months later she swam the same channel, and again fog clouded her view. This time she swam with an image of the shoreline in her mind. This time she succeeded. Not only was she the first woman to swim the Catalina Channel, she beat the men's record by two hours.

The only thing worse than being blind is having sight but no vision.
HELEN KELLER

US Air Force pilot Colonel George Hall was shot down during the late 1960s when the United States was at war in Vietnam. He spent seven and a half years as a POW in a North Vietnamese prison.

Before his capture, he weighed more than two hundred pounds. He lost one hundred pounds while in prison. One week after his release, he shot a seventy-six at the 1973 Pro-Am New Orleans PGA Open—matching his pre-POW handicap of four.

How was that possible?

Every day in prison he played a full game of golf in his imagination. When asked if it was luck, he reportedly said, "Luck, I never three-putted a green in the last five years!"

The power of visualization and imagination is not to be underestimated.

YOUR INVISIBLE TOOLBOX

Devices may be impressive in their capacity to store, process, and compute. These inspiring stories illustrate the impressive power that resides in the mind, equipping humans to tackle overwhelming challenges that no computer invented to date could achieve.

Visualize positive outcomes

93

WHAT MAKES YOU TICK?

The millennial generation has been heavily imprinted with the message that they can be anything they want to be. Is it true?

Of course not. If you're five foot ten, playing in the NBA is not likely in your future, no matter how hard you work at it. If you'd rather have a root canal than spend time converting Fahrenheit to Celsius, perhaps a scientific career is not for you. If you can't carry a tune, your goal to be an internationally renowned singer may need to be tweaked.

Self-awareness allows us to recognize our strengths and weaknesses so we can make good choices in life. Self-awareness is about the "what" and "how." When it comes to interpersonal skills, it's about being in tune with *what* your behaviors are and *how* they may be impacting relationships and outcomes.

Self-awareness is not enough. Self-knowledge is also necessary. It's about the "why" and understanding *why* you are behaving in a certain way.

For example:

- I tend to become aggressive in the face of conflict. This is self-awareness.
- I use an objective, detached approach to decision-making that leads me to jump to debate and judgment in problem solving. I risk overlooking the negative impact my behavior may have on others who use a different approach. This is self-knowledge.

Here's another example:

- I tend to quickly apologize when someone is disappointed or upset. This is self-awareness.
- When faced with potential conflict, my first consideration is the impact on the people involved. My interest in preserving harmony and my dislike for telling people unpleasant things leads me to try to smooth things over too quickly. This is self-knowledge.

From Socratic writings to modern times, the concept of knowing self has played an important role in the pursuit of personal growth. Warren Bennis, professor at the University of California, stated the following in his book *On Becoming a Leader*:

"Knowing yourself is the most difficult task that any of us faces. But until you truly know yourself, strengths and weaknesses, know what you want to do and why you want to do it, you cannot succeed in any but the most superficial sense of the word."

The invisible toolbox is about human interactions. In gaining an understanding of people, it's important to start with self. Until you understand yourself and your strengths and blemishes, you will be unable to maximize the quality of your interactions with others.

Knowing others is intelligence; knowing yourself is true wisdom.
Mastering others is strength; mastering yourself is true power.
TAO TE CHING

Without a clear grasp of what makes you tick and why, you are at the mercy of your seemingly unexplainable reactions. Without a clear sense of who you are, you are unlikely to find fulfilling success in interactions with others. Once you've begun to explore and understand the many facets of your natural tendencies and thinking patterns, you'll be in the position to exercise stewardship over your own behaviors, attitudes, personal strengths, and weaknesses.

YOUR INVISIBLE TOOLBOX

By gaining a deep knowledge of self through reflection, feedback, and assessment, you'll reveal blind spots, discover and build on strengths, and recognize that a strength done to excess can become a weakness. Only then can you begin developing a plan of action to address skill gaps.

Pursue self-knowledge

—————————— 94 ——————————

ARE YOU A MORNING PERSON?

She has appeared on *Time* magazine's list of the most influential people more times than anyone else in history. Her empire is estimated to exceed $3 billion. Versions of her name are now commonly used as verbs to describe a range of behaviors and outcomes.

It wasn't always that way.

She was born in Kosciusko, Mississippi, to an unmarried teenage mother. Raised in poverty, she was taunted in school for her dresses fashioned from potato sacks. Beginning at age nine, she was molested by a cousin, uncle, and a family friend. This led her to run away from home at age thirteen. At fourteen she became pregnant, and the child died shortly after birth. When she tried to talk to her family as a young adult about her molestation as a child, she was doubted.

Her life started to turn around when she was sent to live with her father, who made her education a priority. She became an honors student, joined the high school speech team, and earned a full college scholarship. She won a beauty contest and attracted the attention of a local black radio station where she worked part-time and began her impressive career.

This is the story of Oprah. Oprah Winfrey forever changed the format of interview talk shows that, until she arrived on the scene, were dominated by white males. She is credited for changing the lives of countless viewers of her popular TV show, and the Oprah Book Club is noted for reshaping literary publishing. Few would have bet on the young girl raised in poverty in rural Mississippi to become one of the most recognizable and influential people on the planet.

How does someone with so many disadvantages in early life achieve such impressive success? How can we beat the odds?

According to Greek mythology, Pygmalion sculpted a statue of a beautiful woman. He prayed to the gods that his statue, named Galatea, be transformed into a real woman. His wish was granted. The Pygmalion Effect states that people will respond to how they are treated by others.

The Galatea Effect illustrates the power of self-expectations and self-esteem. It states that an individual's expectations about his or her own performance are a determining factor on ultimate performance. If we think we can succeed, we likely will. If we think we will fail, we likely will. When others hold negative expectations of us, we can overcome those expectations by holding even higher ones of ourselves.

> *Whether you think you can, or you think you can't—you're right.*
> HENRY FORD

When we enhance our self-worth, self-image, and self-esteem, we can trigger the Galatea Effect, which is a powerful method for enhancing performance and achieving success.

Beliefs are things we believe to be true. Do you believe you're a morning person? Or a night owl? How you behave during these times of day is largely a product of your beliefs about yourself. Beliefs are formed throughout your life. Like habits, they're hard to change because you've repeated your beliefs for many, many years.

Many people think they're born with their beliefs. This is simply not true. Beliefs are formed as part of a lifelong conditioning process. They are learned, and they can be unlearned. This is good news for each of us.

Changing your beliefs about yourself can allow you to feel differently about experiences and result in different behaviors that lead to different outcomes, just like Oprah.

YOUR INVISIBLE TOOLBOX

Insights into your core beliefs can help you understand why you feel the way you do about certain situations. These beliefs can limit you from reaching your potential.

Challenge your beliefs

95

DON'T THINK ABOUT IT

They are easily distracted. They expect a trophy just for showing up. They are entitled. They are lazy. They are self-absorbed. These are just a few of the phrases used to describe the millennial cohort. Are these beliefs accurate? Is that how members of the millennial generation see themselves?

What do you think of you? What are you good at? What are you not so good at? What is your self-image? Don't think about what others think of you. What do you think of yourself?

> *No one can make you inferior without your consent.*
> ELEANOR ROOSEVELT

You have many beliefs about yourself. These beliefs control your ability to realize your wonderful potential. When you learn to change these beliefs, you can expand your skills and realize your goals. If you grew up thinking you were shy, then you are shy. If you believe that you are naturally overweight, then diets will only work for you for a short time, and you will gain the weight back.

How we talk to ourselves, our self-talk, has a powerful impact on our lives. Self-talk is the internal conversation we have with ourselves all day long, every day. The beliefs we hold about ourselves are what control the real use of our potential. Over the years, we've been telling ourselves a lot with our self-talk—that we're shy or outgoing, a warm person or a cold one, a high performer or a low performer.

Don't think about a steaming hot piece of apple pie. **Don't think** about the big scoop of homemade vanilla ice cream melting on top of it. **Don't think** about the wonderful cinnamon smell.

It's hard not to think about it, isn't it?

The message just placed in your head is a powerful one, and we did it by telling you what *not* to think about. Your self-talk (negative or positive) is doing the same thing all day, every day for you.

Affirmations are positive self-talk that guide us toward our goals. It is important to affirm correctly or the desired results will not be achieved.

If you go through life focusing on the negative, you prevent yourself from maximizing your personal potential—an insight Mother Teresa tried to pass on to an impassioned group of antiwar protestors. The demonstrators asked Mother Teresa if she would be willing to lead a huge antiwar demonstration. She told them she wouldn't march against war but followed up with an invitation to call her if they ever held a demonstration for peace. When you're against something, you use your creative energy in defense, leaving little energy to create positive outcomes for what you desire.

Does talking to yourself sound like some kind of crazy self-help technique, like standing in front of a mirror and telling yourself you're wonderful and people like you? In some ways, the answer is yes. The important thing to recognize is that it's not a question of if you're going to affirm—you already do. It's whether you're going to do it effectively.

If we want to imprint our children with a good sense of self-esteem and a positive expectation for the future, we can ask these two questions every night. This will cause them to shift their self-talk.

 • What did you do today that you're really proud of?
 • What are you looking forward to tomorrow?

We must stick with it. Our children might think the questions odd at first. Once they get used to the new pattern, they'll talk positively about themselves every day.

Now consider the conversation you have with yourself at night before you fall asleep. Are you telling yourself how proud you are of your performance? Probably not! If you're like most of us, you're likely berating yourself for not getting enough done during the day. This is self-talk, and it's negative. Shift to the positive.

After practicing on yourself and your loved ones, try the technique out on your team. Invite each member of the team to respond to these two questions:

- What are you proud of from your actions last week that moved us closer to our goals?
- What are you looking forward to doing this week that will move us closer to our goals?

Make this a weekly routine and monitor the results.

We build and change our self-image through self-talk. Many of our thoughts are constructive, others are debilitating. The greater our self-image or self-esteem, the easier it is to deal with new situations and challenges.

YOUR INVISIBLE TOOLBOX

It is often said that if a friend talked to you the way you sometimes talk to yourself the friendship would be over in a hurry.

Make positive affirmations

96

THE CONTENT OF THEIR CHARACTER

Most millennials want to know, like, and trust a brand before they buy it. They are less impressed with fancy advertising and packaging and more impressed with the attributes of the product itself. Additionally, they want to know they're dealing with real people, not some faceless corporation. And they want to know the opinions of others they trust.

How do you sleuth out all that information when making a buying decision?

Don't judge a book by its cover, so the saying goes. Sage advice? Perhaps. Practical? Not at all.

Recall the last time you were faced with a multitude of titles on a single subject. How did you cull through the choices efficiently to locate the resource that would serve your purpose? The advice given about not judging a book by its cover is not useful to you in this moment. It's not practical for you to read each book in its entirety or even speed read critical sections to determine which resource you can trust.

You need a shortcut. You narrow the possible choices to a few based on book covers, familiar authors, and recommendations from others. You further narrow your selection by perusing the book jacket to quickly decipher what critics have to say about the contents of the book. If the choices are still too many, perhaps the table of contents gets a look.

Understandably, we take shortcuts.

While few would argue with the beauty of Dr. Martin Luther King Jr.'s dream of a world where people would be judged by the content of their character rather than by the color of their skin, our natural programming makes this unlikely.

We do judge a book by its cover—literally and metaphorically. On the surface, it seems unjust. Practically, it's how we make sense of the world and how we quickly sort through the huge amount of sensory stimuli we encounter throughout the day.

We can't control the filters that others choose when they look at us.
RACHEL WOLCHIN

You can complain all day long about the unfairness of being overlooked for a promotion at work when you perceive yourself clearly more qualified. You can lament the injustice of inequalities you perceive in the workplace that seem connected more to gender, age, race, sexual orientation, disability, or other differences than they do to workplace contributions. Or you can seek to understand your natural filtering system that makes it possible for you to take shortcuts.

When have your unconscious filters led you to reach an erroneous conclusion or make a poor decision? Incorporate this critical knowledge into your invisible toolbox and into your day-to-day interactions.

YOUR INVISIBLE TOOLBOX

Acquiring intelligence and wisdom about your filters can ensure the shortcuts you take don't lead to negative unintended consequences.

Examine your filters

97

TELL ME ABOUT YOUR CHILDHOOD

The members of the generation to which each of us belong share many things. That's where some of the unfortunate and often inaccurate generational stereotypes come from. Isn't there more to you than the fact you are a member of the millennial generation?

Family of origin, the family we grew up in, is where we first learn how to get our needs met, communicate, and process emotions. We acquire a lot of our patterns from this early programming, especially our methods and approaches in relating to others. These early influences can stay with us our entire lifetimes.

Other things change us, but we start and end with the family.
ANTHONY BRANDT

Values and beliefs are often acquired from families. The politics of one's original family are commonly shared—at least for a while. Political inclinations are often evident before an individual has acquired sufficient maturity and knowledge to form an independent view. Religion, attitudes, viewpoints, and philosophies are also passed along through families. Affiliations to sports teams, universities, communities, or people must be traced to family of origin, as evidence is seen of them in toddlers—people far too young to have come to these decisions on their own. Even hatred for specific sports teams or groups seems to be shared in families.

Experiences in dysfunctional families can leave some of their members wrestling with difficulties throughout their lifetimes. For others, the same dysfunction can lead them to make opposite choices in interacting with their own families.

Those who were raised in emotionally healthy environments certainly have an advantage over their disadvantaged peers. However, even functional families can leave harmful marks on their members. Issues that people experience in the present can often be traced back to family of origin influences. Relationship expectations (consciously or unconsciously) may also be held because of interaction patterns from childhood.

Most families are a blend of both positive and negative traits. What is good? What is bad? Those are questions addressed by a different body of research and explored in other books. The purpose here is to challenge you to reflect on your early experiences with family of origin and contemplate how those experiences may have shaped you, your beliefs and values, and your relationships with others.

YOUR INVISIBLE TOOLBOX

What tools in your invisible toolbox may have been acquired through family relationships? Are they serving you well now?

Reflect on family influences

98

MIND THE GAP

All millennials tend to be lumped together. But with such a wide range of birth years, from the early 1980s to the early 2000s, there's quite a gap in age…and expectation?

Millennials on the front end of the cohort feel as if the label "aging millennial" somewhat fits. The differences hit on what all cultural differences highlight, a shared frame of reference. Test yourself on this quiz from a blog by Julie Sprankles. Which side do you resonate with? If these were a continuum, where would you fall?

- Carrie Bradshaw or the Kardashians?
- Prom date or prom proposal?
- Zebra cakes or gluten free?
- Meeting someone in a bar or Tinder?
- Early dial up or Snapchat?
- Spice Girls or Beyoncé?

It's not that you have to like one or another; in fact, older millennials probably relate to both. Those who plotted themselves more on the left side of that list may not be as fluent in understanding everything their 2000-something cohorts do. Younger millennials may not relate to the gen X influence or those millennials who favor the left side of the list above. As blogger Sprankles mentioned, as an aging millennial she's under the same umbrella as those fifteen to twenty years younger and, "That's a big ol' chunk of time, rife with change."

So what is to be learned from this millennial lumping? Frame of reference is a strong influence when it comes to preferences and expectations. As Anais Nin said, "We don't see things as they are, we see the things as we are."

Baby boomer and gen X colleagues have a frame of reference too. It may be difficult to understand where they're coming from because millennials were never there. Boomers who have a challenge accepting flexible working hours might do so because their frame of reference might have been a strict nine-to-five workday. Gen Xers remember pay phones, so they may not be as keen to update technology as quickly as millennials.

Frame of reference is a shared set of understandings, knowledge, and beliefs of a group formed by their common experience. It can be a cultural group, generational group, or family. We cannot know the other person's experience, but remembering what's inside their frame, even if we don't get it, is as important and valid as what is in ours.

YOUR INVISIBLE TOOLBOX

Inquiry about attitudes and habits that relate to frame of reference can help minimize confusion and close the gap of misunderstanding.

Discover your frame of reference

— 99 —

WHO KNEW THAT SHE HAD TALENT?

Millennials are expected to be a powerful generation both in numbers and skills. Their contributions to the workforce are expected to go far beyond maximizing the use of technology. Their experience with the global economic crisis has resulted in them making compromises at a young age, and it's expected that this will translate into a focus on people needs over organizational needs when they assume leadership roles in the workplace. While attending to their interest in a balanced life, millennials are also expected to innovate at an impressive rate and not be restrained by "that's how we've always done it" attitudes in the workplace.

High expectations are the key to everything.
SAM WALTON

On April 11, 2009, a very modest-looking Scottish woman walked out onto the stage of *Britain's Got Talent* television program. Plain in appearance, she did not have the stage presence of someone expected to sing in a way that would bring people to their feet. And yet she did.

Susan Boyle belted out "I Dreamed a Dream" from *Les Miserables*. From that moment, she was an international sensation.

Why?

Researchers have a name for this. It is called the Talking Platypus Phenomenon. It's the notion that we evaluate people not merely on skills and talent but on those factors as compared to our expectations.

In the case of Susan Boyle, there was a disconnect. If her visual image had matched society's expectation of a captivating performer, people's expectations would not have been so wildly exceeded as they were when she arrived to the stage as she did.

Expectations have a huge impact on your own behavior and your interactions with others. What is expected from you?

YOUR INVISIBLE TOOLBOX

People are constantly forming expectations based on what they see. When those expectations are wildly exceeded, the results are long-lasting as illustrated in the story of Susan Boyle.

Exceed expectations

—————————— 100 ——————————

ARE YOU WHO YOU SAY YOU ARE?

"The eyes are very unreliable witnesses. Sometimes they see what they are meant to see."

Hercule Poirot, Agatha Christie's famous Belgian detective, uttered this significant phrase when solving a murder mystery that had captured his attention. He realized, as many of us do, that simply perceiving something does not make it true.

We form perceptions all day every day. Whether checking out the dating pool, interviewing a candidate for employment, evaluating the school district in the area, observing an employee at work, approaching a manager, or sizing up a political candidate, we consult our mental database and form a perception.

How are perceptions formed? What impact do perceptions have on success? Can we influence how others perceive us?

In psychology and the cognitive sciences, perception is the process of acquiring, interpreting, selecting, and organizing sensory information. Relying most heavily on our five primary senses (sight, sound, smell, taste, touch) and to some degree on our sixth sense (gut), we arrange our impressions to form a conclusion—our perception.

In business, perception is reputation.

Everyone knows the story of the man who showed up for an introductory cup of coffee with his Match.com date only to realize that the photo of the individual he was to meet didn't look anything like the woman who was waiting for him.

Or what about the woman who chatted online for months with someone she thought was taller than her and then in meeting him found herself wishing she hadn't worn heels. He had clearly embellished his height on the online profile.

When individuals create their persona for online dating sites, they frequently exaggerate or outright lie on their profiles in an attempt to attract a mate. Misleading virtual identities have become common as more and more relationships develop online.

In face-to-face meetings, physical attributes are obvious, and personality traits start to emerge early in the relationship. In fact, as the relationship develops, the personality traits tend to override the physical attributes as people begin to get to know and relate to one another on a deeper level.

Online dating sites have added an element of mistrust as false identities are able to flourish and remain undetected as long as the relationship stays in the virtual sphere. What do men exaggerate about? Most often they embellish their education, profession, socioeconomic status, and height. What about women? The most common complaint of men who have met women online say it's that women portray themselves as lighter in weight and younger in age.

Is the carefully constructed virtual identity an example of deception or simply descriptive of an individual's ideal self?

Questions about authenticity of online identity are not limited to dating sites. Organizations fall into this trap.

Businesses seeking to create a favorable impression and leverage the vast reach of the Internet often create an online presence inconsistent with the offline experience individuals will have with the organization.

The shortest and surest way to live with honor in the world
is to be in reality what we would appear to be.
SOCRATES

Take the example of booking a hotel online. Perusing the pictures on the hotel's website or the discount travel site leads you to believe you're going to arrive to a beautifully appointed room with every amenity, including a fine dining experience onsite. You imagine and anticipate the look on your partner's face when he or she arrives at this paradise with you.

Unfortunately, your expectations don't match up with your online research. Instead of a beautifully appointed room, you arrive to tired quarters that have seemingly not been updated for decades, evidenced by the stained brown shag carpeting. When you inquire at the front desk about reservations for your fine dining experience, you're informed the hotel no longer serves dinner, and in fact, if you wish to have dinner, you need to get in your car and drive to a different part of the city. Or you can order pizza from the takeout menu they provide.

You instantly realize your credibility is now forever linked with this travel experience, and unfortunately, the dismayed look on your partner's face is the only cue you'll receive for the rest of the evening, because he or she has stopped talking to you. It's not what you imagined.

When reality is mixed and expectations are not met, the results can be catastrophic.

And some of the wounds are self-inflicted, as Anthony Weiner, disgraced member of the US House of Representatives from New York City, found out the hard way. Three sexual scandals related to his own sexting behavior led to his resignation as congressman in 2011 and the breakdown of his marriage in 2016.

Individuals go to a lot of trouble to create an expectation of greatness in their resumes and online profiles. Similarly, companies go to a lot of trouble to create an expectation of greatness either online, with their physical facilities, or in their marketing materials. Unfortunately, it's often forgotten that we must be ready to meet the expectations we create. It's easy to exceed low expectations. If we created an anticipation of greatness, those expectations are high.

YOUR INVISIBLE TOOLBOX

The temptations to (mis)represent ourselves and our organizations as idealized or aspirational versions of ourselves is very high. What happens when we artificially create a perception that we can't consistently meet or exceed? Who we are, what we do, and what we say must all be aligned.

Align online and offline identity

The Original Set of Tools

Since the early stone age, humans have been improving the tools they use. Today's high-tech tools enable us to be more inventive, effective, and efficient than at any time in history.

This pattern of innovation has not been repeated for the tools in the invisible toolbox. In many respects, the tools we use in human relations vary little from the tools our primitive ancestors used. For members of the millennial generation, the wide availability of high-tech tools that has led to impressive productivity and efficiency has also led to the unfortunate unintended consequence of halting (and in some cases reversing) the growth of relationships.

An upgraded invisible toolbox of one hundred tools was presented in this book. Before we conclude our time together, let's examine the twenty-four most common tools we have and the risks of using each. Think of these as the interpersonal tools that came with the original set. As you review them, reflect on these tools as well as your own natural tendencies. Begin to assemble your own personal invisible toolbox, choosing upgraded tools that will help move you most speedily toward your ambitious goals.

1. Accommodation: Accommodation tools are used when we're heavily focused on the people side of a situation. We sacrifice finding the best solution to the problem in favor of preserving harmony in a relationship. This tool is commonly used by those who describe themselves as people pleasers.

When we find ourselves "giving in" to keep peace too often in relationships, we may be relying too heavily on this tool.

2. Aggression: The aggression tool is used when we are focused heavily on goals, eager to win, even at the expense of others, or when we perceive that someone else's win will be a loss for us. This tool is commonly used by those who describe themselves as highly competitive.

When we find our relationships are strained, we may discover that we're sacrificing relationships for results. There are better tools that allow us to preserve relationships and achieve results.

3. Apology: We use our apology tool when trying to restore trust and harmony. When we say "I'm sorry," we're trying to influence the emotional state of the other person so we can explain ourselves or describe the situation. We believe an apology is a useful tool for repairing relationships, eliminating tension, and communicating remorse.

A heartfelt apology is appropriate when we've wronged someone or when our behavior (even unintended) has led to hardship for another. If we use the apology tool for other reasons, we may be over-apologizing when it isn't appropriate, which can be seen as insincere or can set us up to be taken advantage of.

4. Avoidance: When we wish to avoid confrontation, don't want to address a problem, or are concerned that an interaction may potentially damage a relationship, we use the avoidance tool. Retreating from the situation or shutting down and becoming silent is seen as a better approach than risking an argument.

Avoidance is appropriate if either person needs time to calm down and reset. Most of the time it's intended to avoid an uncomfortable situation. In doing so, we're most likely delaying the confrontation until later. Use the advanced tools presented in this book rather than avoid difficult conversations.

5. Blame: This tool is used to point out an underlying reason why a goal was not achieved or a result fell short of desired outcomes. Blame is a self-defense mechanism we turn to when we are part of a task or project that relies on contributions from more than one party to complete.

We like to see ourselves as competent. When faced with a situation where our competence or credibility is in question, it's common to deflect with blame. This book provides better tools to preserve credibility while also addressing the situation directly—which will enhance our competence.

6. Busy: We believe that busy is the badge of honor of all successful people. When we respond to the question "how are you?" with "crazy busy," we're using the busy tool to communicate to others our value and worth. When we notice others relaxing when there's work to be done, we may resent them.

If we equate success with constant and overlapping activity, we may be missing the plot. We must challenge ourselves to reassess what's keeping us so busy and use prioritization skills to ensure we're getting the most important things done, not just getting more done.

7. Compromise: We use our compromise tool when searching for a middle ground between two differing positions. This tool is one we've been taught to use since we were small children. We believe it leads to a solution everyone can live with.

Compromise is a tool that may have a place in our invisible toolbox—just not the first tool we reach for. Searching for mutually beneficial options that meet the interests of all parties before making concessions or asking others to do the same is a collaborative approach that delivers better outcomes.

8. Confrontation: We use this tool when something bothers us or when we disagree. Rather than letting things go, we believe we should confront people and call them out on their behavior or wrong views.

Open discussions about conflict are healthy if handled with effective tools. In most cases confrontations are one-sided and lead to damaged relationships. Before initiating a confrontation, we must challenge our assumptions and examine the situation thoroughly, preferably with the involvement of the other party.

9. Connected: Our connected tool ensures we are always reachable and available to others. We keep our mobile device handy and discreetly consult it whenever we have an opportunity. This helps ensure we don't miss anything important.
Knowing when to connect and when to unplug are advanced tools in the invisible toolbox. The comfort that comes from constant connectedness is small reward when relationships suffer because we don't give them the same priority we give our devices.

10. Decisiveness: We use our decisiveness tool when we are determined, or to seek to put an end to a discussion, or believe that hesitation may have a detrimental effect on an outcome. We make an immediate decision so that action can quickly follow.

We rarely have the whole picture, and the decisions we make in the moment may look different minutes, hours, or days later when more information is known and when unproductive emotions decrease. A good decision is almost always a better outcome than a fast decision. We recognize this is true if we've ever experienced "on second thought."

11. Defense: We use this tool when we feel threatened, criticized, or attacked. We may provide proof that we aren't guilty or argue a point. We seek to protect ourselves through asserting power, demeaning others, or retreating to the comfort of familiar people who agree with us. We build figurative walls to separate ourselves from those we disagree with.

While some threats are real, most are not. Our defense mechanism kicks in when we perceive a threat or when the threat is merely a psychological one. Taking the time to fully appraise the threat before launching into defensive behavior serves us well in long-term human relationships.

12. Denial: We use the denial tool when we find ourselves in an uncomfortable situation, simply can't believe something, or refuse to accept something. We're convinced our belief or approach is the "one right way" and reject anything to the contrary.

Denial may be a safe way to protect the ego, but it's a poor way to foster growth and forward progress. Maintaining an open mind and heart reminds us that there's rarely only one right way to do anything if we're willing to look hard enough for options.

13. e-Communicate: The e-communicate tool is used when we're trying to be efficient, want the opportunity to revise our message before delivery, or try to avoid the emotional discomfort a conversation might bring. We believe e-mail, text, blogs, and social media platforms have revolutionized how we connect with others.

Electronic communication is a speedy and efficient way to connect when relationships are good and misunderstandings are unlikely. When we e-communicate to avoid a conversation, we are hiding from discomfort. We can choose different tools when misunderstandings are possible or relationships may be harmed.

14. Explain: We use our explain tool when asking to be excused for an action we've taken or are required to provide a reason for inaction. We believe an explanation provides justification to others if we've made a mistake, fallen short on an obligation, or are trying to avoid doing something we don't want to do.

Telling our side of the story may feel good, but we rarely learn much by justifying our own actions and views. Before we explain, we can ask open-ended questions to seek to understand the situation more thoroughly.

15. Good intentions: Our good intentions tool is used when our actions have created inconvenience or hardship for others. We find comfort in knowing that our intentions were pure despite the fact that our actions may have resulted in negative outcomes. It's our hope that the injured party will also find comfort in the knowledge that the negative consequences were unintended.

Penalties in the legal system are greater for those with malicious intent. That doesn't release those with good intentions from being held accountable for their actions. While we find comfort in our good intentions, we can't stop there. If our actions cause hardship to another, more is required from us.

16. Honesty: We use honesty when we openly and candidly share our opinions with others. We appreciate honesty from others and

believe we learn and grow from honest feedback. As a result, we are forthcoming with our suggestions, opinions, and perspectives. Honesty is always appropriate when describing how a situation has impacted our own feelings and experience. We must also remind ourselves that honesty may be in the eye of the beholder when we give opinions, advice, or suggestions to others. These may not be welcome. We can seek permission before offering suggestions or wait until we're asked.

17. Listen to respond: We use our listen to respond tool when someone else is talking and we're thinking about what we're going to say in response. We use this tool to engage in a conversation, make important points, and be expedient in problem solving.

Most of us who think we're good listeners are listening to respond. Listening to understand is a much higher level of listening that delivers benefits for everyone. When we listen to respond, we focus on our own goals. When we listen to understand, we focus on everyone's goals, including our own.

18. Multitasking: The multitasking tool is used when we're trying to impress ourselves or others with our ability to handle multiple tasks. We also call on this tool when we want to work at our highest level of productivity or when we have many things happening simultaneously and are confident we can manage them all effectively.

The human brain is a magnificent machine that's designed to focus. Using it as it's designed demands that we focus on one thing at a time. Multitasking has been shown to lead to lower levels of productivity and higher levels of stress.

19. Passive-aggressive: We use our passive-aggressive tool when we feel powerless or want to get even without the risk of confrontation. We combine passive (accommodating) and aggressive (competitive) behaviors. We use sarcasm, guilt, cutting humor, and indirect responses. We may communicate exasperation and impatience nonverbally.

We must remove the passive-aggressive tool from our toolbox permanently. We all occasionally resort to this tool as it's part of basic human programming. It allows us to assert ourselves without engaging in conflict. Yet it's unproductive and responsible for damaging careers and relationships. We can catch ourselves when we fall into passive-aggressive patterns and choose a different tool.

20. Procrastination: We use procrastination when we aren't sure how to start a project, don't like the task, lack confidence in our own abilities, or feel overwhelmed. Either consciously or unconsciously, we look for distractions, interruptions, or something more interesting to do until an impending deadline or mandate spurs us to action.

While it's often thought that laid-back, flexible, unscheduled social types are the only ones who procrastinate, we all do. We can track our procrastination patterns. Do you procrastinate when it comes to leisure and relaxation? Do you delay quiet, reflective introspective thinking time? Do you avoid interactions that may be negative or conflictual? Do you procrastinate when it comes time to make a final decision? Getting to know your own individual procrastination patterns helps you set goals to ensure that procrastination doesn't become a barrier to success.

21. Reward and punishment: We use this tool when we're trying to influence someone's behavior or when challenging them to achieve greater goals. We believe that "what gets rewarded gets done" and that penalties can be powerful motivators of human behavior.

Rewards and penalties, when meaningfully attached to specific behaviors, are appropriate. We now have many more tools in our invisible toolbox to tap into internal motivation and foster an environment where people want to work hard and challenge themselves in pursuit of goals.

22. Snap judgment: Snap judgment is used when we have partial information and feel the need to quickly make a decision or form an opinion. We use our own experiences, standards, and moral compass to size up a situation or action and pass judgment.

It's wise to register our first intuitive reading of a situation knowing it may be right or wrong. Before jumping to a conclusion or making a snap judgment, we can use the questioning tools in our new invisible toolbox and get the facts to validate our first judgment and decide if it's the right one.

23. Telling: We use our telling tool when trying to change someone's mind, provide instructions, or have a point to make. We believe that telling our story or sharing our views leads to greater understanding and can save time in problem solving and decision-making.

Sharing our thoughts and knowledge can be a wonderful gift for others. Unfortunately, our messages frequently fall on deaf ears. Before telling others what we think they need to hear, we can prep them for the interaction by fostering a dialogue about the subject or seek permission to share our thoughts.

24. Trust: We use our trust tool when interacting with others and want to convey confidence. We embrace the philosophy "trust until you have a reason not to." We like to see the best in others and assume they share our values and will fulfill commitments and exercise good stewardship over resources.

Trust is important in all aspects of our lives. It's also earned over time. We should work hard to earn the trust of others while being aware that it's risky to automatically assume trust. When it has been earned, we can reward it. When it hasn't yet been earned, we can create opportunities to build it. When it has been lost, we can learn from the situation.

While it's certainly true that some of the tools listed above are more dangerous and damaging than others, each of them has a dark side. It's a dark side that presents frequently when the individual employing the tool isn't skilled in the use of the more advanced tools presented in this book.

When your apology backfires, when your trust is misplaced, when you find yourself asking how many times you have to tell someone what to do, or when your honest feedback isn't well received, you already know firsthand that something went wrong. It's in these moments that we seek a new approach: the new tools in the invisible toolbox.

We are not recommending that you remove all of the tools listed above permanently from your invisible toolbox. As you read this book, we encourage you to examine each one, polish or sharpen it as appropriate, and relocate it to a place in your toolbox that is less accessible to your reach.

The twenty-four tools listed above should not be the first ones you reach for in interpersonal interactions. When used, they should be used cautiously and in conjunction with other tools presented throughout this book. Pull these tools out after you've assessed a situation. Once you recognize the potential damage the tool can cause, you can make an informed choice.

The invisible toolbox that best equips you for success in the modern economy contains different tools than those that may have been appropriate in the past. It's packed with more advanced tools than the standard invisible toolboxes you've probably been carrying around. With time and practice, they will become your go-to tools once you're skilled in their use. You'll find yourself relying less and less on the rudimentary tools listed above, and your relationships will improve as a result.

Through examining your own interpersonal interactions, you are taking an important step to meaningful growth and change. Congratulations.

Your Invisible Toolbox Reference Guide

Notes

Introduction

Technical skills and knowledge account for about 15 percent of the reason an individual gets a job, keeps the job, and advances in that job. The remaining 85 percent of job success is based on the individual's people skills. Quoted by the Protocol School of Washington, DC, about research conducted by Harvard University, the Carnegie Foundation, and the Stanford Research Institute.

The Council of Economic Advisers, "15 Economic Facts About Millennials," October 2014, 5.

Time magazine, May 2013.

Part I: Tools for Interacting with Others

Chapter 1: It Was One of Those Days

Pew Research Center reports and data on the millennial generation are referenced in this first chapter and throughout the book. http://www.pewresearch.org/topics/millennials/.

CBC Radio Show As It Happens interview hosted by Carol Off, December 2, 2015, http://www.cbc.ca/radio/asithappens/as-it-happens-wednesday-edition-1.3347233/man-dies-24-hours-after-he-pays-for-a-stranger-s-groceries-1.3347240.

Matthew's Legacy Facebook page, https://www.facebook.com/ShareMatthewsLegacy/.

Chapter 2: The Hopeful Generation

Dr. P. M. Forni, Baltimore Workplace Civility Study, 2003.
Forni, Dr. Forni's Civility Web Site, Johns Hopkins University, http://krieger.jhu.edu/civility.

William James, Thinkexist.com, http://en.thinkexist.com/quotation/the_deepest_principle_in_human_nature_is_the/15218.html.

Peggy Tabor Millin, *Mary's Way: A Universal Story of Spiritual Growth and Transformation* (Celestial Arts, 1995).

Chapter 4: The Big Ask

Amit Chowdrey, "Microsoft CEO Satya Nadella Apologizes for Comments on Women's Pay," *Forbes*, October 10, 2014, http://www.forbes.com/sites/amitchowdhry/2014/10/10/microsoft-ceo-satya-nadella-apologizes-for-comments-on-womens-pay/#3a862c7f7300.

"Negotiation Skills Interest Chart," *Tero International Graduate Resources*, http://www.tero.com/graduates_resources.php.

Chapter 5: A New World of Citizen Journalism

David Corn, "SECRET VIDEO: Romney Tells Millionaire Donors What He REALLY Thinks of Obama Voters," *Mother Jones*, September 17, 2012, http://www.motherjones.com/politics/2012/09/secret-video-romney-private-fundraiser.

Emily Schultheis, "Braley on Grassley: A 'Farmer' with no Law Degree," *Politico*, March 25, 2014, http://www.politico.com/story/2014/03/bruce-braley-chuck-grassley-farmer-with-no-law-degree-105010.

Internet archive: Wayback Machine, https://archive.org/web/.

Chapter 6: What Are We Overlooking?

"What Do I Do to Get My Customer to Share Information?" *Tero Tips*, YouTube video, https://www.youtube.com/watch?v=y3TA7VBYmOs.

Chapter 7: May I Make a Suggestion?

"What Are the Three Types of Closed-Ended Questions?" *Tero Tips*, YouTube video, https://www.youtube.com/watch?v=GXIH97CzXOA.

Chapter 8: Instead of Making Your Case

Association for Talent Development, State of The Industry Report, ATD 2015, www.td.org.

"How Can I Direct the Sales Discussion to a Certain Topic?" *Tero Tips*, YouTube video, https://www.youtube.com/watch?v=W5DDLtQ5Gc4.

Chapter 9: What Is Your Edge?

Ilan Mochari, in *Inc.com, Edge Strategy: A New Mindset for Profitable Growth* by Alan Lewis and Dan McKone (Harvard Business Review Press, 2016).

Chapter 11: Say It Again, Sam

Elaina Zachos, *Technology is Changing the Millennial Brain,* November 15, 2015, public source.

Dr. Kirk Erickson, Brain Aging and Cognitive Health Lab, University of Pittsburgh, http://www.pitt.edu/~bachlab/LabSite/Home.html/.

Oprah Winfrey, www.oprah.com.

Chapter 12: Whether You Like It or Not

Dr. Harwant Khush, "Tips and Techniques to Work with Verbal Criticism," Tero International, Inc. articles and publications, http://www.tero.com/article_verbalcriticism.php.

Dr. Mark Gorkin, *Going Postal and Beyond: Part One,* http://www.stressdoc.com/going_postal_i.htm.

Chapter 13: I Don't Understand What You're Saying

John Brandon, "15 Words and Phrases Millennials Use but No One Else Understands," *Inc.,* September 11, 2015, www.inc.com, http://www.inc.com/john-brandon/15-words-and-phrases-millennials-use-but-no-one-else-understands.html.

Chapter 15: How Are You Guys Communicating?

Howard Gardner, *The Art and Science of Changing Our Own and Other People's Minds* (Harvard Business Review Press, 2006), 164–168.

"What Are a Few Examples of Communication Gone Wrong?" Tero Tips, YouTube video, https://www.youtube.com/watch?v=3oWtlqHM0Ug.

Chapter 16: Friend or Foe

PON staff, "How Snap Judgments Can Lead Bargainers Astray in Negotiations," *Harvard Program on Negotiation,* October 17, 2016, http://www.pon.harvard.edu/daily/dealing-with-difficult-people-daily/how-snap-judgments-can-lead-negotiators-astray-in-negotiation-conversations/.

Chapter 19: Tend to Your Net

Joe Girard, *"Girard's Law of 250" (blog)*, March 1, 2014, *https://www.joegirard.com/posts/girards-law-250/*.

Chapter 25: Are Things Really What They Seem?

Walter Lippman, *Communicating Globally, Intercultural Communication and International Business* (Sage Publications, 2007), 33.

Chapter 26: You Have a Choice of Airlines

Ibid. See reference to Protocol School of Washington, DC, research cited.

Chapter 27: #Winning

Nick Shore, "Millennials Are Playing with You," *Harvard Business Review*, December 12, 2011, https://hbr.org/2011/12/millennials-are-playing-with-you.

Part II: Tools for Presenting Yourself in the World

Chapter 29: Caught on Camera

Niall Jenkins, "245 million video surveillance cameras installed globally in 2014," *Building Technologies*, IHS Markit Technology, June 11, 2015, https://technology.ihs.com/532501/245-million-video-surveillance-cameras-installed-globally-in-2014.

Vince Lattanzio, "Woman Violently Abducted off Philadelphia Street Found Alive, Vicious Predator Arrested," *NBC News,* November 6, 2014, http://www.nbcphiladelphia.com/news/local/Abducted-Woman-Found-Alive-in-Maryland-Police-Source-281698261.html.

Chapter 31: The White House Crashers

Wikipedia, 2009 US state dinner security breaches, https://en.wikipedia.org/wiki/2009_U.S._state_dinner_security_breaches.

Albert Mehrabian, *Silent Messages* (Wadsworth, 1971), 286, 305. See also http://www.kaaj.com/psych/.

"Frank Abagnale Biography," *Biography.com*, http://www.biography.com/people/frank-abagnale-20657335#synopsis.

Dr. Robert Cialdini, *Influence: The Psychology of Persuasion* (Harper Business Review, 2006), 227.

Chapter 32: Look Me in the Eyes

Evan Marc Katz, *Can You Fall in Love by Simply Holding Eye Contact?*, http://www.evanmarckatz.com/blog/understanding-men/can-you-fall-in-love-simply-by-holding-eye-contact/.

Chapter 34: Who Smiled First?

"Smiling – one of the more philanthropic things you can do! It activates your life force and others!" *Esoteric Online*, March 4, 2012, http://www.esotericonline.net/profiles/blogs/smiling-one-of-the-more-philanthropic-things-you-can-do-it?id=3204576%3ABlogPost%3A492324&page=2.

Chapter 36: Give It to Me Quick

The Protocol School of Washington, DC, Dorothea Johnson, founder.

Chapter 37: Two Seconds to Success or Failure

David G. Jensen, "Tooling Up: First Impressions – Are Interview Results Preordained?" *Science,* August 2004, http://www.sciencemag.org/careers/2004/08/tooling-first-impressions-are-interview-results-preordained. Malcolm Gladwell, *Blink: The Power of Thinking Without Thinking* (Little, Brown, Time Warner Book Group, 2005), 86–87.

"Image and Influence: Polishing Your Professional Look," Tero International, Inc. www.tero.com, Becky Rupiper-Greene, senior image consultant.

Micah Solomon, "2015 Is the Year of the Millennial Customer: 5 Key Traits These 80 Million Consumers Share," *Forbes,* December 29, 2014, http://www.forbes.com/sites/micahsolomon/2014/12/29/5-traits-that-define-the-80-million-millennial-customers-coming-your-way/#144201a2a81f.

Chapter 38: Ditch the Dress Code

Ibid. See reference to Image and Influence, Tero International, Becky Rupiper-Greene, senior image consultant.

Chapter 39: What's Up with Your Voice?

Olga Khazan, "Vocal Fry May Hurt Women's Job Prospects," *The Atlantic*, May 29, 2014, http://www.theatlantic.com/business/archive/2014/05/employers-look-down-on-women-with-vocal-fry/371811/.

Emily Tess Katz, "Vocal Fry, Made Famous by Kim Kardashian, Is Making Young Women Less Hirable," *Huffington Post*, November 3, 2014, http://www.huffingtonpost.com/2014/10/31/vocal-fry_n_6082220.html.

Jeannie Campbell, "Improving Your Vocal Quality," Tero International, Inc. articles and publications, http://www.tero.com/graduates_activity_improving-your-vocal-quality.php.

Diane Di Resta, "Uptalk Speech Patterns May Be Sabotaging the Careers of Women," *Di Resta Communications*, January, 2011, http://www.diresta.com/in-the-media/press-releases/uptalk-speech-pattern-may-be-sabotaging-the-careers-of-women-nationwide/.

Penny Eckert, "Upspeak To Vocal Fry: Are We 'Policing' Young Women's Voices?" *NPR Fresh Air* interview, July 23, 2015, http://www.npr.org/2015/07/23/425608745/from-upspeak-to-vocal-fry-are-we-policing-young-womens-voices.

Reena Gupta, Osbourne Head and Neck Institute website, http://ohni.org/dr-reena-gupta/.

Naomi Wolf, "Young Women, Give Up the Vocal Fry and Reclaim Your Strong Female Voice," *The Guardian*, July 24, 2015, https://www.theguardian.com/commentisfree/2015/jul/24/vocal-fry-strong-female-voice.

Chapter 40: Finding Your Voice

Ibid. See reference to Tero International article, "Improving Your Vocal Quality" by Jeannie Campbell.

Nalini Ambady, Ph.D., Debi LaPlante, MA, Thai Nguyen, BA, Robert Rosenthal, Ph.D., Nigel Chaumeton, Ph.D., and Wendy Levinson, MD, surgical outcomes research, "Surgeons' Tone of Voice: A Clue to Malpractice History" (Boston, Riverside, CA, and Toronto, 2002), http://emerald.tufts.edu/~nambad01/surgeons%20tone%20of%20voice.pdf.

Chapter 41: You Won!

Dr. Harwant Khush, "Accepting an Award," Tero International, Inc. articles and publications, http://www.tero.com/article_award.php.

Chapter 43: The Message and the Messenger

Sandy Thompson, global planning director, Young & Rubicam, "The Secret to Making Millennials Fall in Love with Your Brand," *Huffington Post* blog, September 8, 2012.

James Kouzes and Barry Posner, *The Leadership Challenge,* 5th ed. (John Wiley & Sons, 2012), 38.

Part III: Tools for Working Globally

Chapter 44: Hungry for a Big Mac

David Zanoni, "McDonald's Cultural Adaptability to Bring Continued Success, Seeking Alpha," http://seekingalpha.com/article/855441-mcdonalds-cultural-adaptability-to-bring-continued-success.

Joseph Schumpeter, "McDonald's, The Innovator," *The Economist,* June16, 2011, http://www.economist.com/blogs/schumpeter/2011/06/fast-food-and-cultural-sensitivity.

Chapter 45: Can I Eat French Fries with My Fingers?

Amy Sung, "What Millennials Want," *FSR* magazine, *Food Newsfeed*, May 2013, https://www.foodnewsfeed.com/fsr/what-millennials-want.

Chapter 46: Tricking Human Nature

Kyoung-Ah Nam, John Condon, "The DIE is Cast: The Continuing Evolution of Intercultural Communication's Favorite Classroom Exercise," *Journal of Intercultural Relations*, August 2009, http://global.wfu.edu/files/2015/02/DAE-Article_NamCondon_IJIR_2010_v34.pdf, 81–87.

Chapter 48: Jumping into the Pool

Edward T. Hall, *The Silent Language* (Anchor Books, 1973), reissue.

Chapter 49: The Fast Track

Nancy Adler, *International Dimensions of Organizational Behavior*, 5th ed. (Thompson Learning, Inc. 2008), 44–59.

Chapter 50: Where in the World Are We?

Terence Brake, *Where in the World Is My Team?* (Jossey-Bass, 2007), 188.

Mitchell R. Hammer, Milton J. Bennett, Richard Wiseman, "Measuring Intercultural Sensitivity: The Intercultural Development Inventory," *International Journal of Intercultural Relations*, http://www.sol.lu.se/media/utbildning/dokument/kurser/ENBC11/20112/Hammer_article_Task_1.pdf, 27.

Chapter 51: Getting the Mix to Work

Alex Halperin, "CNN asks if Korea's Hierarchical Culture Caused Crash," *Salon.com*, July 10, 2013, http://www.salon.com/2013/07/10/cnn_asks_if_koreas_hierarchical_culture_caused_crash/.

Chapter 52: The Everyday Diplomat

Eric Heyl, "Millennials: Diplomacy over Force," *Tribune-Review*, July 11, 2015, http://triblive.com/opinion/qanda/8674203-74/millennials-think-china.

Part IV: Tools for Leaders

Chapter 53: The Shoulders of Giants

Author unknown, "Earning Your Desk," *Inspire21.com*, http://www.inspire21.com/stories/truestories/EarningYourDesk.

Chapter 54: Righting a Wrong

Rev. Al Sharpton, "Federal Judge Pushed for Prisoner's Release," *MSNBC PoliticsNation*, July 3, 2016, http://www.msnbc.com/politicsnation/watch/federal-judge-pushed-for-prisoner-s-released-717796931690.

Chapter 56: The Heart Is Where the Enthusiasm Is

Stephen Valbracht, president, Marshalltown Aviation, owner, Midland Aircraft.

Stephen R. Covey, *The 7 Habits of Highly Effective People*, (Simon & Schuster, 1989, 2004).

Chapter 57: Enough Helping Hands

"Track Inspector's Good Deed Goes Viral," *Inside Track*, Union Pacific employee newsletter, August 5, 2015, http://www.up.com/aboutup/community/inside_track/josh-cyganik-8-05-2015.htm.

Chapter 58: What If I Can't Make a Difference?

William Grimes, "Robert Ebeling, Challenger Engineer Who Warned of Disaster, Dies at 89," *New York Times*, March 25, 2016, http://www.nytimes.com/2016/03/26/science/robert-ebeling-challenger-engineer-who-warned-of-disaster-dies-at-89.html?_r=0.

Howard Berkes, "Breaking News From NPR, 30 Years After Explosion, Challenger Engineer Still Blames Himself," *NPR Interview*, January 28, 2016, http://www.npr.org/sections/thetwo-way/2016/01/28/464744781/30-years-after-disaster-challenger-engineer-still-blames-himself.

Chapter 60: Do You Look Honest?

James Kouzes and Barry Posner, *The Leadership Challenge*, 5th ed. (John Wiley & Sons, 2012), 34.

Chapter 61: Not the Trusting Type

Chris Cillizza, "Millennials Don't Trust Anyone. That's a Big Deal." *Washington Post*, April 30, 2015, https://www.washingtonpost.com/news/the-fix/wp/2015/04/30/millennials-dont-trust-anyone-what-else-is-new/?utm_term=.99e42581d4b2.

Joseph and Edna Josephson Institute of Ethics (2012), *Josephson Institute Report Card on the Ethics of American Youth*, www.josephsoninstitute.org. To learn more about the Josephson Institute's Report Card Survey on the Ethics of American Youth, please see: www.charactercounts.org.

Chapter 62: A Sign of a Healthy, Active Brain

"Millennials More Likely to Get Scammed than Boomers," Better Business Bureau, August 17, 2016, http://www.bbb.org/columbia/news-events/news-releases/2016/08/bbb-millennials-more-likely-to-get-scammed-than-boomers/.

Romeo Vitelli, Ph.D., "When Does Lying Begin?" November 11, 2013, https://www.psychologytoday.com/blog/media-spotlight/201311/when-does-lying-begin.

Chapter 65: Look…a Squirrel

Kevin McSpadden, "You Now Have a Shorter Attention Span Than a Goldfish," *Time*, May 14, 2015, http://time.com/3858309/attention-spans-goldfish/.

Chapter 67: Why Didn't You Tell Me?

"Emotional and Psychological Trauma: Causes and Effects, Symptoms and Treatment," *Healing Resources.info*, http://www.healingresources.info/emotional_trauma_overview.htm.

Chapter 69: Why Is Change So Hard?

William Bridges, Ph.D., *Managing Transitions: Making the Most of Change* (Da Capo Press, 2009).

Chapter 71: The Law of the Pack

Jason Gots, "Zappos Will Give You $3000 to Get Your Priorities Straight," *Bigthink.com*, http://bigthink.com/inside-employees-minds/zappos-will-give-you-3000-to-get-your-priorities-straight.

Chapter 73: The Pygmalion Effect

Chad Brooks, "Frequent Job Hopping Not Just a Millennial Trait," *Business News Daily*, April 1, 2015, http://www.businessnewsdaily.com/7889-job-hopping-boomers.html.

Rowena Crosbie, "The Pygmalion Effect," *IowaBiz.com*, Business Record business blog, March 2015, http://www.iowabiz.com/2015/03/the-pygmalion-effect.html.

Chapter 74: The Label Game

"A Class Divided," *PBS Frontline*, March 26, 1985, http://www.pbs.org/wgbh/frontline/film/class-divided/. See also http://www.janeelliott.com/.

Chapter 75: Let's Get Back to Work

David Kahn, "Tag Archives: Wharton Center for Applied Research. Four Ways to Add Value Through Meetings," *Leadersayswhat.com*, April 7, 2015, http://www.leadersayswhat.com/tag/wharton-center-for-applied-research/.

Chapter 76: Gains in Productivity

Tim Hindle, "The Hawthorne Effect, Adapted from 'The Economist Guide to Management Ideas and Gurus'," *The Economist*, November 3, 2008, http://www.economist.com/node/12510632.

Chapter 77: A Canopy Open to New Sunlight

Joel A. Barker, futurist, author, lecturer, filmmaker, www.joelbarker.com.

Chapter 78: It's All Possible

Leslie Scrivener, "The Marathon of Hope," *Toronto Star*, September 1, 1980, http://www.terryfox.org/TerryFox/The_Marathon_of_Hope.html.

Chapter 79: Whose Life Is It Anyway?

Sarah Boxer, "Charles M. Schulz, 'Peanuts' Creator, Dies at 77," *New York Times,* February 14, 2000, http://www.nytimes.com/2000/02/14/arts/charles-m-schulz-peanuts-creator-dies-at-77.

Margalit Fox, "Richard Graham, Equal Rights Leader, Dies at 86," *New York Times,* October 8, 2007, http://www.nytimes.com/2007/10/08/us/08graham.html.

Anne Kisselgoff, "Nathalie Gleboff, Director of School of American Ballet, Dies at 88," *New York Times,* October 8, 2007, http://www.nytimes.com/2007/10/08/arts/08gleboff.html.

Part V: Tools for Personal Growth

Chapter 80: Send in the Clowns

A. J. Willingham, "What's Up with All the Clowns Everywhere? 6 Legit Possibilities," *CNN.com*, October 10, 2016, http://www.cnn.com/2016/10/05/health/creepy-clowns-rumors-trnd/.

Linda Rodriguez McRobbie, "The History and Psychology of Clowns Being Scary," *Smithsonian .com,* July 31, 2013, http://www.smithsonianmag.com/arts-culture/the-history-and-psychology-of-clowns-being-scary-20394516/.

Chapter 81: Stressed Out

Caroline Beaton, "8 Habits That Make Millennials Stressed, Anxious and Unproductive," *Forbes*, February 18, 2016, http://www.forbes.com/sites/carolinebeaton/2016/02/18/8-habits-that-make-millennials-stressed-anxious-and-unproductive/#10b2db44d615.

Chapter 82: Top Floor Thinking

Wikipedia, US Airways Flight 1549, https://en.wikipedia.org/wiki/US_Airways_Flight_1549.

Diavolo, http://www.diavolo.org/.

Chapter 83: Lessons from the Playground

"One-third of Full-time Workers Globally Say Managing Work–Life Has Become More Difficult – Younger Generations and Parents Hit Hardest," *Ernst & Young Global Generation Research*, May 5, 2015, http://www.ey.com/us/en/newsroom/news-releases/news-ey-one-third-of-full-time-workers-globally-say-managing-work-life-is-difficult.

Shawn Johnson – Olympic gold medalist and entrepreneur, http://shawnjohnson.com/.

Michael Phelps – Most decorated Olympian in history, https://www.olympic.org/michael-phelps.

Chapter 84: The Myth of Multitasking

Gary Keller and Jay Papasan, *The ONE Thing: The Surprisingly Simple Truth Behind Extraordinary Results* (Bard Press, 2013), 43–44, 48.

"Multitasking: Switching Costs," *American Psychological Association*, March 20, 2006, http://www.apa.org/research/action/multitask.aspx.

Chapter 86: It Costs Nothing, Unless It Works

James Clear, "The Ivy Lee Method: The Daily Routine Experts Recommend for Peak Productivity," *Huffington Post*, June 2, 2016, http://www.huffingtonpost.com/james-clear/the-ivy-lee-method-the-da_b_10257938.html.

Chapter 87: There is Always More to the Story

"Heart Touching True Story that Happened in Canada," *AV Media*, January 10, 2014, http://avmedia.info/blog/heart-touching-true-story-that-happened-in-canada/.

Chapter 88: Sweat the Small Stuff

Martin Bashir, "Walt Pavlo: The Visiting Fellow of Fraud," *ABC News,* January 30, 2006, http://abcnews.go.com/Nightline/Business/story?id=1557957. Wesley Higgins, "Former White-Collar Criminal to Share Crooked Past," *The Oracle*, University of South Florida student newsletter, October 9, 2014, http://www.usforacle.com/news/view.php/850941/Former-white-collar-criminal-to-share-cr.

Alice Schroder, *The Snowball: Warren Buffett and the Business of Life* (New York: Bantam Books, 2009).

Richard Carlson, *Don't Sweat the Small Stuff and It's All Small Stuff: Simple Ways to Keep the Little Things from Taking Over Your Life* (Hachette Books, 1996).

Chapter 89: Success without Force

Parelli Natural Horsemanship – Horse Training, http://www.parelli.com/.

Chapter 90: Practice Makes Permanent

"The Rotarian Conversation with Itzhak Perlman," *The Rotarian*, November 2009, https://books.google.combooks?id=18YOtenWo5wC&pg=PA50&lpg=PA50&dq=itzhak+perlman+as+a+child+I+hated+to+practice&source=bl&ots=3OQ8Jg5haL&sig=gWQFfWdo J1SYyqljwNLTlRe2WFM&hl=en&sa=X&ved=0ahUKEwiWitzfjrTRAhVJ92 MKHWSYALQQ6AEIPzAI#v=onepage&q=itzhak%20perlman%20as%20a%20child%20I%2hated%20 to%20practice&f=false.

Chapter 91: In the Zone

Zack Pumerantz, "The Strangest Lucky Charms in Sports," *Bleacher Buzz*, June 20, 2012, http://bleacherreport.com/articles/1263785-the-strangest-lucky-charms-in-sports.

Chapter 92: More than Luck

Florence Chadwick story, http://www.queenofthechannel.com/florence-chadwick.

Colonel George Hall story, http://www.consistentgolf.com/mind-control-for-golf-improvement/.

Chapter 93: What Makes You Tick?

Warren Bennis, *On Becoming a Leader*, 4th ed. (Basic Books, 2009), 34.

Chapter 94: Are You a Morning Person?

"Oprah Winfrey Biography," *Biography.com*, http://www.biography.com/people/oprah-winfrey-9534419#synopsis.

"Oprah Winfrey Biography," *Encyclopedia of World Biography*, http://www.notablebiographies.com/We-Z/Winfrey-Oprah.html.

Chapter 96: The Content of Their Character

Dr. Martin Luther King Jr., "I Have a Dream Speech," https://www.youtube.com/watch?v=3vDWWy4CMhE.

Chapter 98: Mind the Gap

Julie Sprankles, "27 Things Older Millennials Remember That Young Millennials Don't," *Bustle*, April 2016, https://www.bustle.com/.../157836-27-things-older-millennials-remember-that-young-.

Julie Sprankles, "10 Things Older Millennials Don't Understand About Younger Millennials," *Bustle*, May 2016, https://www.bustle.com/articles/159670-10-things-older-millennials-dont-understand-about-younger-millennials.

Chapter 99: Who Knew That She Had Talent?

Britain's Got Talent, YouTube video of Susan Boyle's performance, April 11, 2009, https://www.youtube.com/watch?v=RxPZh4AnWyk.

Tero International, Inc.

Since 1993, Tero International has dedicated itself to understanding the abstract personal and interpersonal skills that lead to success in the modern workplace and the new economy. Members of the Tero Team invest thousands of hours in research, program design, and curricula development to translate the abundant and complex findings of research scientists into relevant, practical, and enjoyable training programs that make a real difference to the bottom line for its clients.

Today there are more than fourteen research-based training programs focused on the skills in the invisible toolbox that are so specialized that it requires a team to facilitate. No member of the Tero Training Team is certified to lead all of the programs offered by Tero.

Effective training programs are only part of the solution. Great content in the hands of a poor facilitator does not produce desired results. Certified Tero facilitators, who themselves have received hundreds of hours of training and development to become skilled in the nuances of effective delivery and expertise in learning, lead these state-of-the-art training programs at locations around the world.

Valuable lessons and insights have been acquired on the journey. In addition to helping others learn, Tero has been the beneficiary of much learning as well. What we have learned has shaped Tero's assumptions, beliefs, and philosophy about learning, training, and executive coaching. Most importantly, it has helped the clients we serve bring higher levels of skill and effectiveness to their own business pursuits.

In this book, we have compiled and shared many of these insights. Most of the lessons challenge commonly held beliefs. Many are counterintuitive. All are backed by credible research and have been tested by experience in the real world. All of them together form a recipe for success in human development and organizational success.

Not surprisingly, when mastery of the skills in the invisible toolbox is gained, organizations are not the only beneficiaries. The applications translate to all situations that involve human beings. Relationships in homes and communities also benefit.

Best of all, these tools are all within your reach. Making the effective use of these tools a top priority is one of the best investments you can make in your personal and professional success.

Index

Made in the USA
Columbia, SC
14 February 2019